Healing the Universal Family

Alan Billups P.T.

Copyright © 2010 by Alan Billups PT

Lotus Health Systems, Inc
8639B 16th street #138
Silver Spring, Maryland 20910
www.LotusHealthSystems.com

Overview

This book integrates the relationship between the 7 circuits of brain function, energy healing techniques, and the principle teachings of Nichiren Daishonin, Hermes Trismegistus of Egypt and Shakyamuni of India and has a primary objective to define and illustrate the methodology of how healing the 1st four circuits of brain function creates the foundation for establishing the universal family. The secondary objective is to give a basic template of the teachings of Nichiren Daishonin and how the manifestation of one's Buddhahood is the highest phase of healing (spiritually) for humanity in this day and age.

Each individual will need to develop an awareness of the 7 circuits of brain function to walk the steps toward immortality in the physical dimension, which is a state of life free from spiritual, psychological and physical disease. The current life styles and belief systems on the planet provide the framework for the current manifestations of disorder and disease that the majority of humanity experiences in their daily lives.

Today's time period was defined by Shakyamuni Buddha, the Sage of India, as Mappo, (The Age of Conflict) which began 2000 years after his death on February 15, 949 B.C.

The relationship with the true self can only begin with becoming all that we have been created to be. The foundation of humanities path back to the original self begins with healing the incomplete circuits of the brain, which is the intent of the above teachers.

Acknowledgment

Special thanks are given to the following individuals who have influenced me and inspired me in the compilation of this work.: first and foremost, my father Aaron Billups, who initiated me on the path of spiritual learning and development through his example as a great Buddhist teacher; the many brilliant teachers, which include Dr. Jewel Pookrum, Barbara Ann Brennan, John Baines (Dr. Dario Salas Somers), Dr. Michael Powers , the late Dr. Mona Harrison and all the Nichiren Shoshu Priest who helped me deepen my understanding of the Buddha's true intention and spirit; and lastly Dewey Thomas, who specifically requested that I compile this written work.

Contents

This book will demonstrate how healing works to bring completion to the first 4 of 7 circuits of brain function. The individual's childhood forms the template of right and left brain development, which most often is disrupted by inadequate nurturing to stimulate balanced integration of the right brain and emotional body in the formative years. As an adult this natural brain integration no longer spontaneously happens, which now requires other techniques to address and correct the left brain dominance and dysfunctional behavior of humanity. Doing this sets the foundation for creating the universal family. This book also covers the topic of the psychological aspects of an individual as outlined in Core Energetics, advanced psychology and the role true Buddhism plays in the purification of the six sense organs, which releases the constraint held on the 9th consciousness (enlightenment).

Introduction

    Healing the Universal Family 1

I.   The First 4 Circuits of Brain Function 3

    A. 1st circuit

    B. 2nd circuit

    C. 3rd circuit

    D. 4th circuit

II.   Three Phases of Each Circuit   6

    A. Requirements to complete a circuit

        1. The Role of the Mother

        2. The role of the Father

        3. The role of Information

    B. Consequences of an Incomplete Circuit

        1. General societal patterns and examples

        2. Behavior patterns in individuals

- C. Chemical Triggers
- D. Overview of the 7 circuits

III. Brain Circuits and Core Energetics   17

- A. Characterology wounding: 1st, 2nd, 3rd circuits
- B. Heart space and contact with others- 4th circuit
- C. Circuits of transfiguration- 5th, 6th, 7th circuits
- D. Effects of healing on the circuits
- E. Support for self empowerment- 3rd circuit
    1. The cerebellar- "bird's eye" view of reality
    2. Intellectualism is not conclusive to being humane
- F. The Heart space and wisdom
    1. Animals vs. Human beings
        a. Wise Love
        b. Corrupt Love
    2. The Buddha nature
        a. Kyo Chi Myogo
        b. Kosen Rufu
        c. 8th circuit- amala consciousness

IV.   Dynamics of Healing   20

- A. 4 Dimensions of Human kind

1. The Physical
   a. Western Medicine
   b. Newtonian Physics

2. The Aura
   a. Mental Functions
   b. Personality

3. The Hara
   a. Molten core
   b. Tan Tien
   c. Soul Seat
   d. ID Point

4. The Core Star
   a. Amala Consciousness
   b. Life Pulse
   c. Essence

B. Ichinen Sanzen
   1. The Ten Worlds
   2. The Ten Aspects

C. The Three Poisons

D. Six Causes of Illness

V. **Nichiren Daishonin's Teachings**   **36**

A. Juzu Beads

B. The Three Proofs

C. Law of Cause and Effect

VI. Tools for Healing   55

A. Role Relationship

    1. Male Role

    2. Female Role

    3. Contest

    4. Productivity

B. Kechimyaku

    1. Entity of The Law

    2. Faith

C. The four P's

D. Comprehensive Healing Plan

E. Chanting and the 9th consciousness

VII. The Subjective Realm   80

A. The Brain Functions

B. The Negative Syndrome

C. The Positive Aura

D. The Five Personality Patterns

E. Overview of The Ten Worlds

Glossary   97

Bibliography   132

Chapter 1

Introduction

The universal family is the natural relationship connecting each individual to parents, marital partners, children and siblings that, is referred to as when expanded, includes links to all people and cultures on a global scale. The unique path to completing the healing process out from each individual exists in the fundamental similarities that each of us has in common. The 7 circuits of brain function provide a framework from which an individual can objectively change his subjective interaction with reality via the progression of brain development through each complete circuit. "Based on one's neurological development there are as many realities as there are aspects of the brain for transcending signals."[1] In human growth and development, the natural progression of the brain's development is disrupted due to the lack of understanding about how family, environment and belief systems work in relation to creating the condition of full awareness within a maturing individual.

The foundation of healing based on completing the 7 circuits of brain function can be summarized through the insight of the mind-body interaction.

---
[1] (Jewell Pookrum M.D., 1999)

The mind is an electromagnetic field of energy which encompasses the physical body. In some instances it is called the human aura or bio-energy field. The mind contains our unconscious and conscious thoughts, consequently the cells of our body being permeated by the mind field always know our thoughts and desires.

"It is the brain's function to transform the energy frequency of the mind's contents into a chemical substance (neurotransmitters) that the cells of the body can interpret and respond to. When the chemical translation of our consciousness (mind) is toxic to the cells of our body, we create and experience dis-ease."[2] Hence, surgically removing the tissue of the body which internally responds in a toxic manner to the neurotransmitters made from our conscious mind brings temporary relief, but does not eliminate the true source of the problem, aberrant thoughts.

Consciousness is defined as energy received by structure, and intelligence is defined as energy transmitted by structure. For the human being, the structures are neurocircuits (brain/ central nervous system) and their anatomical connections.[3] Reality is energy registered by neurostructure. This is another way of asking, "How much of reality or truth can we take in?" We "see" only what we are ready instrumentally and conceptually to receive. " Seeing" here can mean perception through each of the five senses of touch, taste, hearing, smell and sight.

___

[2] (Ibid, Pookrum)
[3] (Ibid, Pookrum)

The First 4 Circuits of Brain Function

The first four circuits are of primary importance because the majority of humanity gets trapped in these particular circuits , this happens for numerous reasons, some of which are intentional and others due to pure ignorance. Each circuit corresponds to a different level of evolution and an increasing degree of brain function, which can be translated as an increase in harmonious relations with self and others. This explanation of the importance of complete maturation of the brain's function to the individual and society as a whole, is the foundation of true social order. Anatomically, each of the first 4 circuits relates to specific characteristic behaviors seen in a particular species of animal or insect that will give deeper insight into the circuit into which an individual or group is locked .

The 1st circuit corresponds to the brain stem. The brain stem's function corresponds to the nervous system and consciousness of the reptile. Specifically, this means that we inherently can do what reptiles can do, including regenerate limbs. The problem that arises from this state of consciousness is that an individual will "see" the world around him as the reptile does. The reptile has only two concerns: what is safe, and what is not safe. Reptiles only come together for two reasons only, defense and reproduction. Individuals who are trapped in 1st circuit mentality deal with their reality based on this type of awareness. The individual is always preoccupied with personal safety and competition for survival. The typical male-female relationship has no foundation in trust secondary to fear (safety) being predominately an emotional boundary, along with only pure attraction relating to the sexual drive instinct. Across society, these types of relationships are becoming the norm, and they are short lived. Fighting and the sexual drive become the foundation of the individual's life when he is trapped in the 1st circuit. Protecting homes, cars and our overall best interests becomes an obsession. As in the animal kingdom, the most dominate individuals win the carcass.

The 2nd circuit corresponds to the area just inside the skull, along the region where the Pons are located. This circuit's function can be found to correlate with the behavior of insects, specifically ants and bees. In this circuit, an individual recognizes that coming together as a group to perform tasks creates a greater benefit for all, than if one acted alone. Group effort and contract underline this circuit's function. The problem with this level of neurological development becoming the prominent behavioral expression is that the individual's life and role becomes defined by the group. In short, the contract with the group gives his life meaning. The individual's personal needs and perspectives become secondary to his relationship with the group. A person, for example, would value the functions of his religious organization or job over the importance of his home life or personal health. As with insects, once one defines himself and his role, he is committed by contract, and he cannot break that relationship or he will be killed or removed from the group. Insects have no emotional bond to each other and do not know what compassion is. Insects must be willing to sacrifice themselves for the perspective of the group. Each individual functions under the agreement and guidelines for the survival and advancement of the hive. Insects feel a need to attack others, even though there is enough space on the earth for everyone to coexist, because of the limited view of reality that they have. Humans who are stuck in 2nd circuit brain function see reality from 8% of brain capacity. People in the armed forces are examples of this circuit's function.[4]

The judicial system exists because insects have to have a way to regulate the contracts between each other, so that differences can be modulated. Once an individual defines them self in the role of an insect, they cannot move above or beyond that role for life.

The 3rd circuit of brain function corresponds to the cerebellum, which relates to the capacity of the bird. Birds are the only animal with exception to the ant eater that can deal with the aggression of ants. What is unique to the perception of the bird over the ant is their ability to see the bigger picture. Birds can see the world from an expanded view in the air, a lack that the ants exhibit in their aggressive behavior towards others to protect their space. The expanded view that the bird has corresponds to more information. In humans this is the behavior of the intellect, which represents the ability to better navigate one's life, with the acquisition of more information. An individual stuck in this circuit can only believe something if it has been documented or proven by someone who represents an authority figure. This circuit still represents a

---

[4] (Ibid, Pookrum)

limited capacity of brain function and leads to numerous problematic circumstances in human relationships that are mediated by the left brain.

The 4th circuit corresponds to the lower primates and the ability to feel others feelings. This is the circuit that relates to the heart space or the astral level of the energy field (4th level). This level of perception brings higher justice and integrity to the dynamics of human relationships. True healing can only happen between people when the heart space is involved.

The Three Phases of each Circuit

Each circuit has three phases that must be completed for an individual to mature correctly, and that if a circuit is not completed in the appropriate sequence of development, the individual will spend the rest of their life returning back to the incomplete circuits.[5] A person can move into other circuits prematurely for many reasons. This can be seen in children who are forced to grow up early taking responsibility in difficult family situations. Each circuit has an infancy, childhood and adulthood phase. Mastery of the circuit requires the individual to move through each phase in the same way the individual developed and matured in relation to his or her physical body's function and performance. Naturally infants cannot function in an adult world at the basic survival level

---

[5] (Ibid, Pookrum)

and are dependent on others at this state of development. This gives rise to the role of the parents in relation to the natural progression through the first two circuits.

The mother's role in relation to the baby's natural neurological progression relates to the 1st circuit, which is during the first 2 ½ years of development. Her primary role is to provide;

1. A sense of safety through protecting the child.

2. Nurturance with love and nutrition for emotional and physical development.

3. Give the sense of value to the child, so they develop a sense of self worth. The 1st circuit can only be completed when these three requirements are met.

The father's role is related to completing the 2nd circuit. It is through the child's relationship with him that they develop the capacity to interact with others, based on guidelines and agreements for the survival and advancement of the hive, society. It is his role to give directions toward keeping the order of society; The Law keeper or Alpha male. The child develops self definition in relation to their life purpose, and what it is they are to do in the world.

Information is necessary to move into and develop the 3rd circuit. If an individual lets the role of societal norms serve as the source of their down load of information, he or she will be left at the adolescent/ childhood level of 3rd circuit development. In general, information gives the individual a tool to better navigate their life. The down load of wrong information is the beginning of many dysfunctions within an individual's life.

When a person is exposed to information, there is a neuro-chemical response released within the brain relative to the objectivity of the truth or lack of it within the information. When exposed to a particular truth, the cells within your body ultimately feel or know its relationship to this neuro-chemical translation as being a completely harmonious state of existence relative to how they were created. Therefore, if you ignore the truthful information, you will eventually experience discomfort from within your body until you comply with its truth, or the cells will progressively move into aberrant cell chemistry, known as dis-ease. From this stand point it can be seen how bad information or communication leads directly towards dis-ease. This also relates to telling lies or speaking untruths. If the 4th circuit is open, telling a lie will be felt in every cell of your body as a painful experience. The individual listening to the lie will also be informed by his or her cells that the information being presented is not of the truth. The first 3 circuits deal with mastering one's experience of planet Earth or terrestrial life.[6]

The 4th circuit opens with the heart. However, this relates to wanting to feel one's self and others. In society there is a strong intention of not wanting to feel. Most of the drugs used by people and their overall behaviors lead to specifically avoiding the objective truths that surround them that appear to be unpleasant to experience. This closes the 4th circuit. It is important to note that feeling is a requirement to begin to open circuits 4 through 7. The opening of the 4th circuit is the first step towards living in the truth of the unitive state, the realm of non duality.

---

[6] (Ibid Pookrum)

The environment is also very important to opening up the circuits. The environment that resembles the childhood atmosphere, works to continue the active traits that prevent spontaneous maturation of the undeveloped circuits. This includes objects such as books, religious items, clothing, people and living conditions in general. And that to clean up one's environment half way works to support the activation and clearing of incomplete circuits. The environment and information always exerts an influence on an individual, which they may not be able to overcome relative to the information they have on aboard.[7] From this stand point the suppressive environmental images of the childhood, creates the feeling response neuro-chemically that locks the individual in a particular circuit. From the psychological perspective this is known as transference.

There are also chemical triggers that affect the circuits. These chemicals can be use to open or lock individuals in a particular circuit. These chemicals take the form of foods and drugs. Opiates and heroin lock you into 1st circuit mentality, the reptilian brain function. Alcohol locks you into 2nd circuit behavior, the insect level of brain function. Coffee, speed, high protein diets and cocaine work to lock you in 3rd circuit function, the "bird brain" or intellect. Marijuana opens up the 4th circuit along with other digested carbohydrates. Ibogaine is a drug discovered in a tribe of Mali, that opens circuits 1 through 5 and totally breaks the addiction to all other drugs with one dose in 80% of the recipients, leaving the individual spiritually aware of their purpose in life.[8]

---

[7] (Ibid, Pookrum)
[8] (Ibid, Pookrum)

There are specific behaviors exhibited by individuals and society when individuals are purposely or negligently stuck in particular circuits. Individuals stuck in 1st circuit issues exhibit low self esteem in relation to not having a self worth established by the mother. Lack of nurturance in love and food creates the behaviors of stealing, hoarding and co-dependence on others for survival. Fears, phobias and avoidance develop from the lack of sense of safety being established with the mother.

If an individual moves into relationship with other people (2nd circuit) in society the above conditions become apparent. The 2nd circuit cannot be mastered until 1st circuit issues are resolved for this reason. In society 2nd circuit is exhibited in relation to the judicial system, because ants (people stuck in 2nd circuit) have to have a way to regulate contracts when they are broken or not agreed to, for modulation of the differences. An individual's contract is the role he is obligated to play in his relation to the hive (society), and in some cases marriage. Corporations, government and all team sports are examples of 2nd circuit reality. In insect reality you are killed or removed from the nest (fired) if you violate the specifics of your role in the hive. Insects do not have compassion or feelings towards each other. Everything is contract and commitment to them. The alpha male is the director within the 2nd circuit structure.

The intellectual individual uses information to manipulate and control others. It is interesting to note that birds "the intellectuals" are the only animal capable of keeping the ants in check (society). Ants can invade and take over the space of any other land animal with the exception of the ant eater.

People who move to 4th circuit prematurely, find them self to be dysfunctional and confused about their appropriate orientation in society. Individuals who use marijuana often fit this definition and have an easy going attitude towards practical and serious life issues.

Some people are born with their 5th circuit open, which relates to ESP or high sense perception. A person with this circuit open realizes that they are the entire galaxy, and can see the bigger picture for them self. These people have a difficult time relating to society with this direct access of information. It is important to note that feeling is the key to opening 4th through 7th circuits. This person finds a lot of conflict with the experiences they have and the acceptability of this perception being validated by society, as opposed to 3rd circuit information that is validated by figures of authority. The 6th circuit opens in relationship to accessing the information contained in your body at the level of the DNA and the skeletal system.[9] This circuit is located in the occipital lobe of the brain. It is here were your cells tell you your relationship to all other things in existence and what it is you are to do in your highest manifestation to that reality if activated. There are 12 strands of DNA that most people only assess ¼ of one strand of DNA throughout their life span. Like a computer, some files of DNA are automatically accessed and others need to be down loaded for activation. Seven generations of information about what it is we are to do as a cultural value system is accessed here in the 6th circuit, carried by the DNA of an

---

[9] (Ibid, Pookrum)

individual. The bones of the skeletal system also hold the information about planet Earth in crystalline form, just like a computer's memory banks.[10]

The 7th circuit corresponds to the frontal lobe of the brain and is where an individual has the capacity to rewrite one's script on how they have been wired to function in this lifetime. Some of the programs there that are not desirable can be removed. These programs may be in the form of bad habits or inherited disease processes carried over from generations prior. Each individual is hardwired to behave a particular way based on the specific influences surrounding their birth, otherwise known as your astrological sign or imprinting. There are 13 specific ways an individual can be imprinted to function in this dimension, explains Dr. Pookrum. "It is at the level of the 7th circuit that one has the ability to transform themselves. It is here that the full expression of the God and Goddess within an individual can be actualized. This is the level of 100% brain function and the state of immortality in the physical dimension. At this level of brain activity the cells of the body receive the highest level of neuro-chemical stimulation that provides them with the necessary environment to continually regenerate."[11]

Within the universe it is obvious that time and friction wears things out, however we human beings have the regenerative properties that reside in the frontal lobes of the brain and can therefore experience immortality in the physical form based on these laws. Being in truth is the primary requirement for

---

[10] (Ibid, Pookrum)
[11] (Ibid, Pookrum)

this type of existence, because anything that was created to exist in this dimension was design to function in that capacity. Yet, as humans we have the choice to act accordingly or not. If we do not behave in accordance with the truth or laws of this life, we are unable to access the amount of life force or consciousness needed to activate the frontal lobes of the brain, the 7th circuit. Dr. Pookrum states that the basic structure of our nervous system is similar to that of a tree, some of which are thousands of years old. In nature there are many reminders of how we can continue to exist on a divine level, if we are willing to change. As an individual progresses through and completes each circuit, the brain releases the neuro-chemistry relative to that level of brain function, which is proportionate to the increase in life span.

Dr. Pookrum states that there is a tribe in Africa that has individuals who regenerate lost limbs within 11 years, which is a somewhat de-evolutionized aspect of this property within humans secondary to their poor dietary habits. The 7th circuit is being actualized in the western sciences as genetic engineering, which appears to be an aberrant form of cellular regeneration based on 3rd circuit mentality.

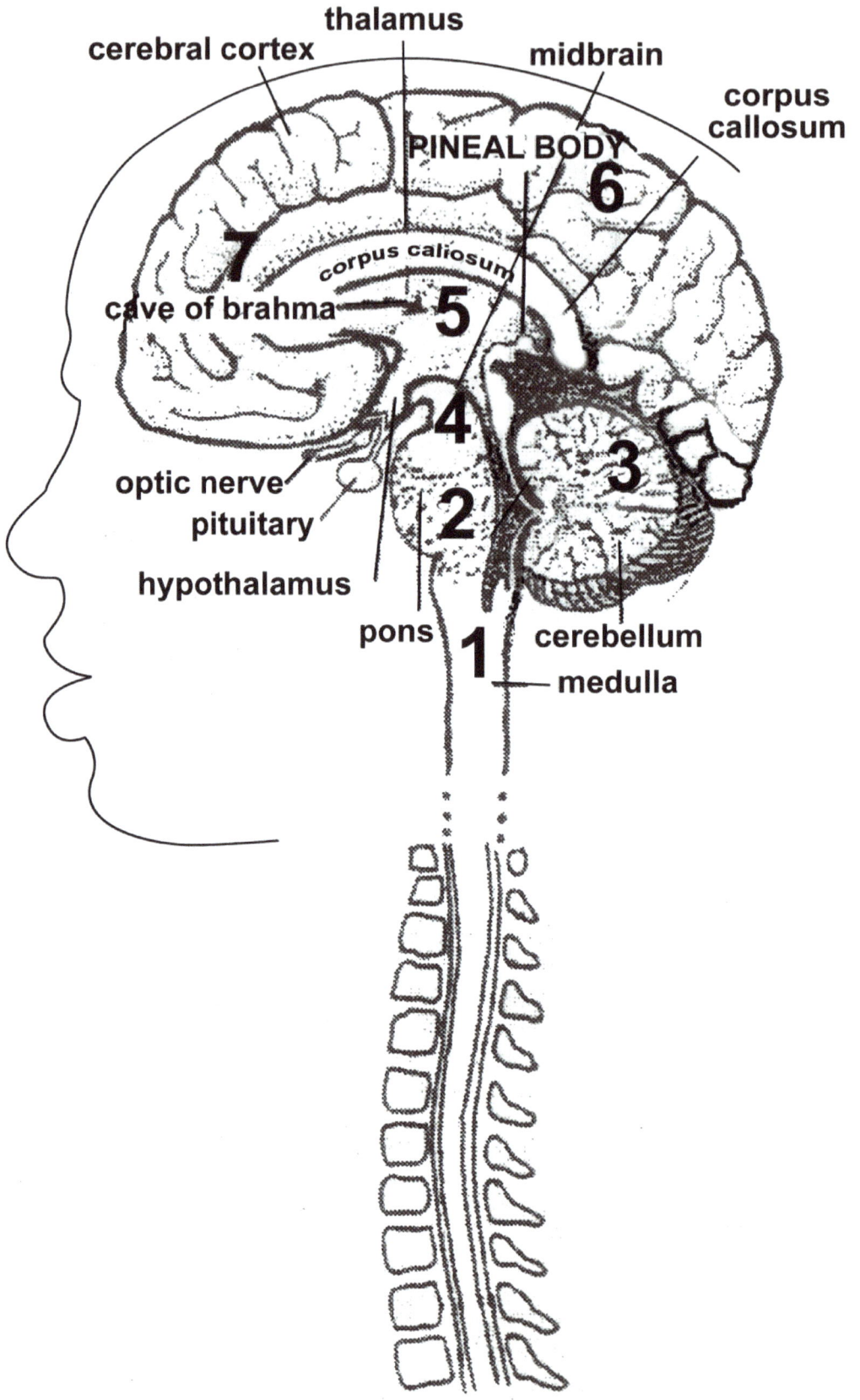

Fig. 1

The 7 circuits of the Brain

Overview of the 7 Circuits of the Brain

*1st circuit- The Brainstem which is the oldest part of the brain, evolved over 5 hundred million years ago. Since it resembles the entire brain of a reptile, it has been referred to as the reptilian brain. It regulates the general level of alertness and warns the organism of important incoming information, as well as handling basic bodily functions necessary for survival.

*2nd circuit- the area of the Pons and the Fourth Ventricle, which is tuned to the storage of experiences within the social dimension of our physical environment. The Pons give us a more refined memory than the immediate physical sensation and make us act together with a behavior similar to the herd instinct of most animals and seeking of group protection.

*3rd circuit- the Cerebellum area, which contains all our lower emotional responses and governs the coordination of all lower functions, including special acts concerned with range, direction, rate of force of movement, and the synchronization of physical organs. This part of the brain has the capacity for analysis and comparison so that whenever we have a experience that we can compare, it randomly scans the lower brain structures by picking out sensory information and emotional responses, since it has the ability to use the two lower brains at the same time. It makes us able to use all the logical and comparative sequential methods of analysis and to compare, contrast, differentiate and organize. Third circuit-based rationalist fear people who are demonstrating intuition. The response to a problem, when viewed by someone who has dominance in this circuit is to "reason it out," The rational realist.

4th circuit- the Mid-Brain, hypothalamus, the thalamus and the floor structure of the inter-brain. This part of the brain determines our evolution or stagnation and is the key to the control over our fluctuating identity. The function of the 4th brain regulates the energy of the life force through the chakras when they are open. If the 3rd brain does not redirect the energy of the life force through itself "The intellectual experience of life" the individual can begin to identify with the correlation between consciousness and matter. The 4th brain controls the gateway to the higher structures of the brain which can supply energy (life force) or cut it off at will. Without the life force switched on to the higher centers in the brain, the individual's spiritual being stays asleep. When people rooted in this circuit confront a problem it is usually transmuted into guilt and involves a "moral" solution.

5th circuit – composed of the Inter-Brain the Third ventricle and the Cave of Brahma. This part of the brain allows us to experience devotion or higher types of love not analyzed by our emotions. It is here were we are able to bring together and compare many concepts and patterns of higher emotions forming judgments of how life should be and making models and estimates of reality. The level of the brain which integrates ideas and where the nervous system begins to direct the body, it is the circuit of bliss that can work to heal disease. It is estimated that when 51% of the population reaches function of this level of brain circuitry great social changes will evolve on the planet.

6th circuit- consist of 3 lobes on the left and right sides of the cerebral hemisphere, which contain the Parietals, used for inner vision, the Occipitals which govern our sense of sight and focusing on sighted objects and the temporal, which governs and arranges our conceptual speech, our listening and our physical balance. It is this part of the brain that joins concepts together holistically from all of our sensations from the separate senses acting together, giving us the feeling of knowing. It is the level of intuition, where we are able to know without forming concepts. Individuals begin to have premonitions that later manifest in apparent coincidences. This is the initial phase of awakening, to the experience of higher consciousness out of the normal perceptions of the lower consciousness.

7th circuit- the frontal lobes, where there is a perception of infinite realities. The brain becomes aware of itself within a creative void, which represents cybernetic consciousness where the programmer begins to program himself.[12]

---

[12] (Valerian, 1992)

Brain Circuits and Core Energetics

There are many similarities between the 1st four circuits and the 5 characterology types illustrated in Core Energetics. It can be clearly seen that the 1st circuit issues relate to the schizoid and oral characters, which have their definitive issues around existential fear and nurturance. The psychopathic issue relating towards controlling others and its aggressive nature is a trait of the 2nd circuit. The masochist needs to feel and express self along with dependence are also conditions of being locked in 2nd circuit. The intellect (3rd circuit) often has difficulty believing in a spiritual reality and is very rational to the point of not accepting any objective proof outside of what is authorized to be real by western science. The intellect falls within the description of the rigid character.

The schizoid individual's main fear is living in a human body as an individual, because they experienced direct or perceived aggression. Energetically this person leaves their body, resulting in its physical weakening and their tendency to vacate during threatening situations. This person needs to surrender to being human and learn to experience their individuated essence. The oral person fears not having enough of anything relative to physical and emotional nurturance. At an early age they experienced lack of nurturance and abandonment; resulting their inability to metabolize energy from the environment and their use others as the source of their energetic, physical and psychological nutrition. This person needs to experience their individuated essence as an infinite source within and learn to nurture themselves as being enough.

The psychopathic individual's main issue is betrayal. Their experience was being used and betrayed by someone or something very close to them. They deeply fear letting go and trusting, which leads them to control others in the form of aggression. Inside this person is a hidden belief that their essence is bad or evil, so when in aggressive conflict with others, winning out over the other is perceived as a struggle to remain good; which leaves all others in the position of the evil one that opposes what is right. This cycle must continue until this person begins to truly trust others and allow their own mistakes and still be safe. They must begin to recognize and honor the core essence and higher will of others around them, without the need to control them.

Masochistic individuals have experienced being controlled, invasion and theft resulting in humiliation. The resulting effect on this person's psyche is dependence and the inability to differentiate between self and others. To heal this person needs to be free to feel and express self, learning most importantly how to say no to others. These individuals tend to hold their energy and inner feeling within, causing it to build up and then be released in anger. Continual expression of their feelings is the method needed to clear the underlying issue of the masochist.

Rigid individuals cannot experience the authentic self they posses inside, because they were in denial of their psychological and spiritual reality during early development. They deeply fear imperfection so they act appropriately rather than authentically. These people must put themselves into life and feel the real self in its current day to day reality.

Chapter 2

Dynamics of Healing

To begin the clear process of healing oneself, it is necessary to have a complete understanding of the creative process as it exists in life. Nichiren Daishonin elaborated on this point when he said, "If you don't know the nature of a person's illness, the only thing you will do is make it worst." [13] Knowing the nature of how the dynamics of a human being's life process unfolds is key to unlocking the root source of the true inherent cause of dis-ease on the physical, emotional, mental and spiritual levels of one's life.

Barbara Brennan has illustrated the 4 dimensions of humankind throughout her extensive work within the Universal Energy Field, that permeates all life and the environment. She defines the 4 dimensions of Humankind as being composed of the physical level of reality, the auric field; the haric level and the core star (essence).[14] Healing takes place on many levels of reality (fig 2). However, most people are concerned only about what becomes obvious to them on the conscious level where a noticeable imbalance can be distinguished through pain or emotional and physical dis-ease. The true illness

---

[13] (The Gosho Translation Committee, 92)
[14] (Brennan, Light Emerging, 1993)

in humanity is always found at a much deeper level of reality than is apparently observable to the individual's five senses.

If one were to observe the phenomena of the glass of water with sediment at the bottom, he or she would develop a keen description of the process of healing and disease in their current life situation. As one observes the glass undisturbed, it would appear that the liquid content is pure. However, if one were to stir the liquid in the glass, the seemingly pure content would become deluded with the sediment residing at the bottom of the glass.

In a person's life the sediment at the bottom of the glass corresponds to the inherent cause of illness or dis-ease. The inherent cause corresponds to ignorance and the karma that a person holds latent in their 8th consciousness. The 8th consciousness is referred to as the Karmic repository, located below the realm of conscious awareness. It is where all karmas created in present and previous lifetimes are stored. Named the alaya-

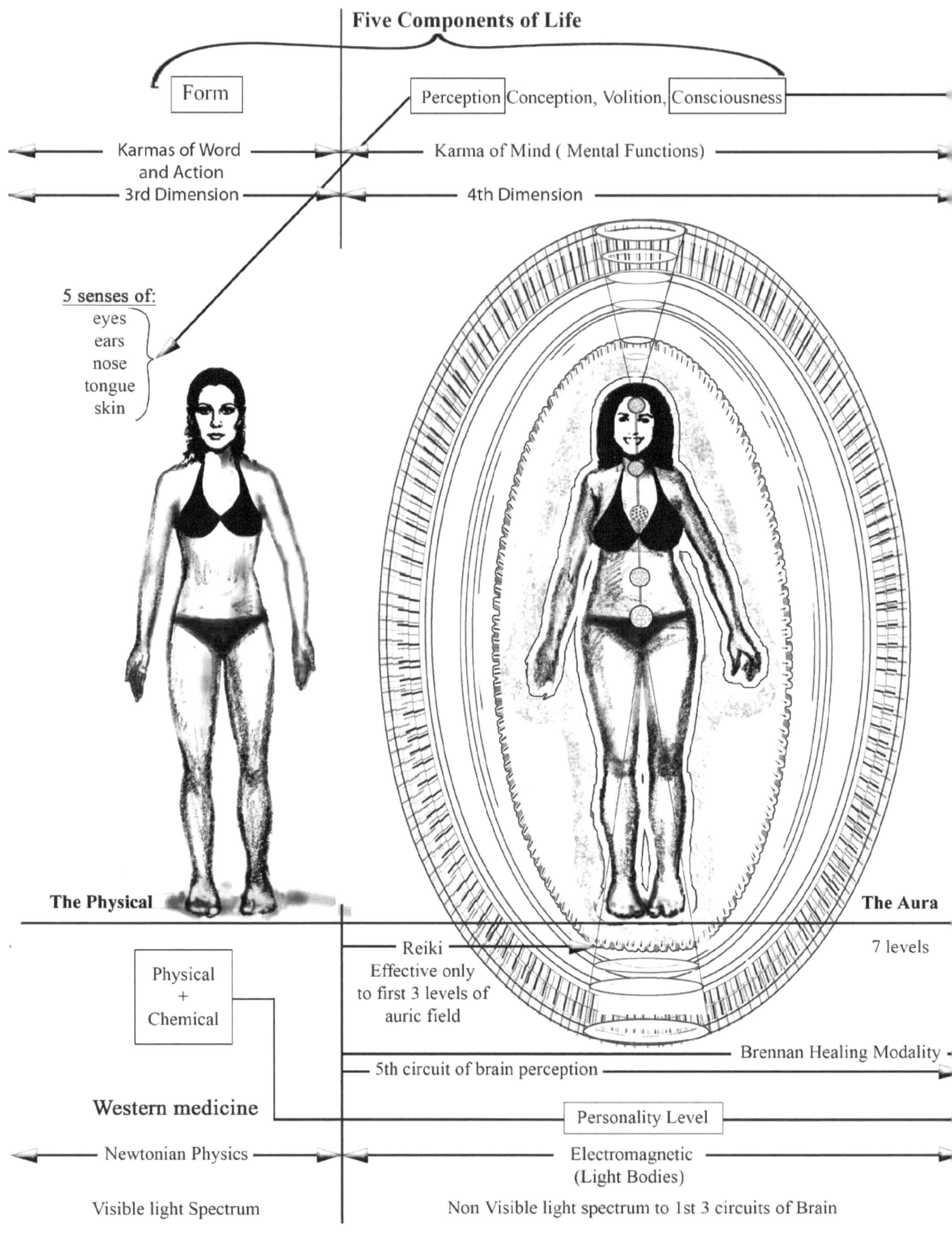

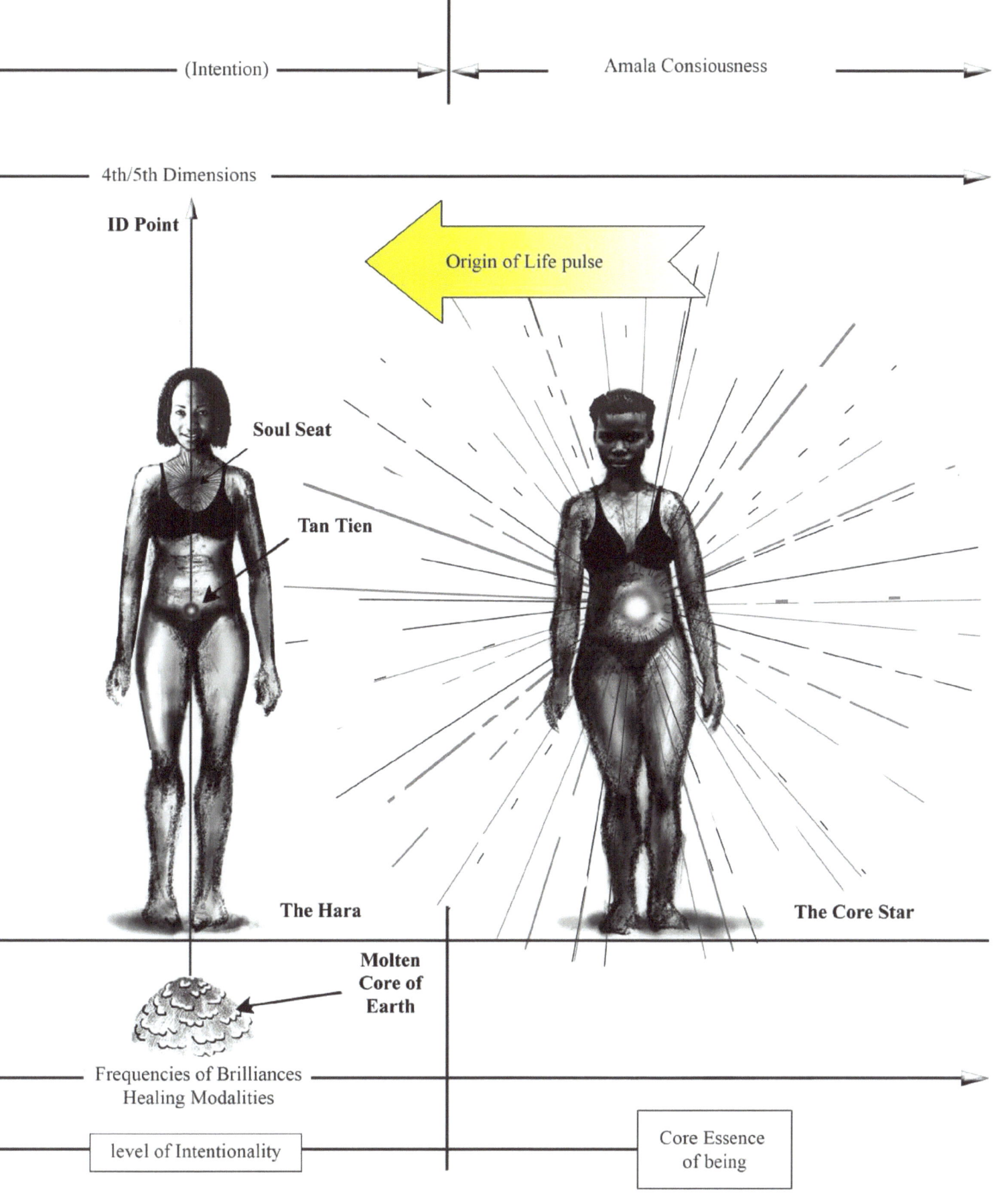

Fig. 2

4 Dimensions of Human Kind

consciousness, it is regarded as that which undergoes the cycles of birth and death and forms the framework of individual existence. The various distortions and blocks that are observed by a trained healer in the Human Energy Field correspond to the inherent illness within the mind or auric field. The actions of life bring forth the apparent dis-ease state only when the correct cause and conditions come together. Energy is the catalyst for all reactions to come to completion. Time X energy equals power. There has to be a sufficient life power to activate the inherent nature of the disease process on the deepest level. The environment has an influence on the majority of such unfolding conditions in the human experience of dis-ease. The principle of Ichinen Sanzan gives a complete yet complex view of how this reality unfolds in its most profound aspect.

Buddhism's core and most profound principle is Ichinen Sanzen, which literally means 3000 realms (sanzen) in a single moment of life (ichinen) experienced by a person's mind. Myoho Renge Kyo is actual Ichinen Sanzen in the complete sense of the concept, because it is the manifestation of all phenomena (shoho jisso).

To develop an understanding of what Ichinen Sanzen is, the explanation and illustration of what Nam Myoho Renge Kyo is will be useful. Nam is a Sanskrit word meaning to devote one's life. In the Ongi Kuden Nichiren Daishonin explains, "In the phase 'to devote (ki) one's life (myo),' ki indicates the physical aspect of life, and myo, the spiritual aspect."[15] In Buddhism this is

---

[15] (The Gosho Translation Committee, 92)

called shiki shin funi (the oneness of mind and body) or the entity of a person's life.

Myoho translates to mean mystic law. Myo being the life essence or ichinen, the unfathomable nature of life which is beyond words or concepts. If a person tries to conceive of no existence or reality what so ever, he will find that it is beyond his mind's power to hold the idea of absolute nothingness in his being. As opposed to the same awareness of everything and all time as it manifest and un-manifest throughout infinite myriads of possible forms of expression throughout the known and unknown universe. This aspect of life is beyond comprehension and is the fundamental meaning of Myo.

Ho of Myoho is the phenomenal manifestations of reality that manifest as absolute or law. The parallel to this aspect can be seen in the first law of thermodynamics (physics), which states that matter and energy can neither be created nor destroyed. Hence, this law (ho) has no beginning or end as we know it, and is eternally the fundamental truth of life as it expresses itself in all phenomena we observe. This is the core of the fundamental truth that all Buddhas of the past, present and future come to realize and through their correct subjective relationship to it (Kyo Chi Myogo) expressing the three enlightened properties of the Law (the truth of life's spiritual and physical nature fused into one thing-entity), wisdom (the correct subject relationship to that truth-mental or spiritual nature) and action (the correct behavior in relationship to the truth- one's physical actions or deeds). Ho and Kyo in this sense are fundamentally the same thing, objective truth. Ho therefore corresponds to the meaning of sanzen, how the phenomenal world manifests in 3000 realms. (Fig. 3)

Renge represents the principle of cause and effect, and is the expression of how this law manifests throughout time and space (environment). From a subjective standpoint related to the individual's actions (causes) and results from those actions (effects), this is known as the principle of Karma.

Kyo is the mind of the Buddha or the truth which he expresses from his mind in the words he speaks. Therefore kyo can be sound (words) or the reality we see, as it manifest in all phenomena as the nature of the law itself displaying cause and effect (shoho jisso).

This forms the platform from which we can begin to understand the full meaning of what Ichinen Sanzen is. The number 3000 is derived by multiplying the 10 worlds x the mutual possession of the 10 worlds x the 10 factors x the 3 realms.

To begin we must explain what each concept means. The 10 worlds are life conditions that an entity of life manifests from moment to moment with changing conditions. The 10 worlds are hell, hunger, animality, anger, humanity or tranquility, and rapture or heaven, which compose the lower 6 worlds. These worlds work in close relation to the power and influence of the environment that a person is experiencing. Learning, realization, bodhisattva

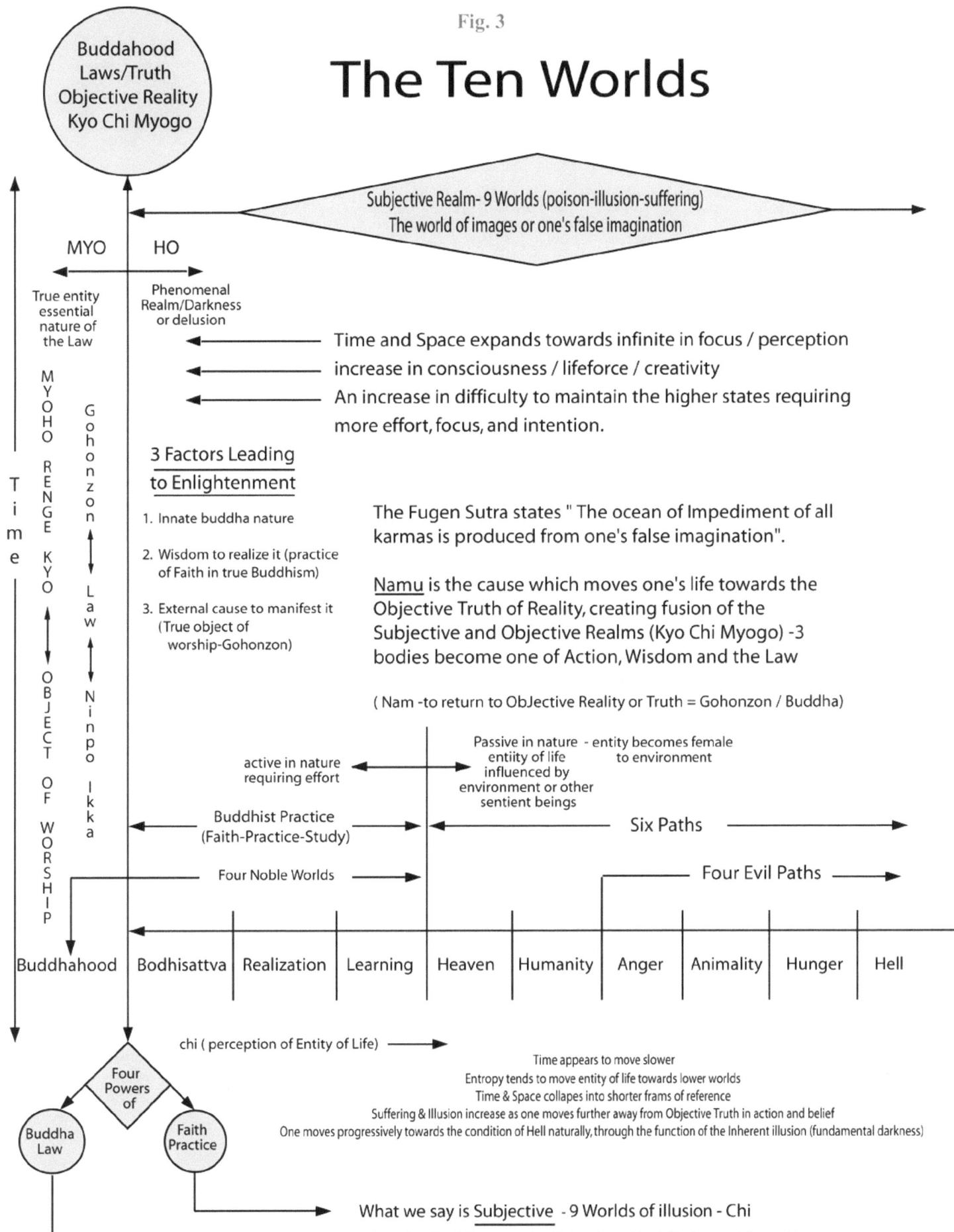

Fig. 3 — The Ten Worlds

and Buddhahood compose the 4 noble worlds and require individual effort to maintain oneself in them.

The 10 aspects or factors of life are 1.appearance (form and color of all things), 2.nature (spiritual properties of one's mind and all things), 3.entity (the fusion of body and mind that forms the person's complete being or the physical and spiritual aspects of all things), 4.power (the energy of a person's life that allows him to act a specific way in each of the 10 worlds); this power is either originating from within or outside the individual, leading to the next factor under which the person is either the source or object being influenced. 5. Influence (the volitional activities of words, thoughts and actions that are characteristic of which world the person is in; i.e. Anger or Hunger). The next 4 factors are related to the concept of time, were as power and influence correspond to space and its energetic and dynamic properties. The first 3 factors are related to life itself. 6. Internal or inherent cause is one's karma and is the seed of the experience a person will have when the right cause and condition manifest for an effect to occur. Example: if a person has a predisposition to get skin cancer (inherent cause), he must be in the right condition for this potential to manifest (external cause); in the sun on a very hot day for an extensive amount of time. 7. External cause being the next factor that corresponds to influence from the environment or other sentient beings. 8.Latent effect is the reaction to the phenomena internally by the individual to the manifested effect which is the skin cancer that was produced by the stimulation of the inherent cause (karma) by the environment (external cause), which produces the 9.manifested effect (observable outcome of a person's past actions-causes). 10.

Consistency from beginning to end. Beginning corresponds to 3.entity and end corresponds to 9.manifested effect (in Buddhism this is called actual proof) or the results of one's actions in life (benefit or suffering as the result of correct or incorrect religious belief). Another way to look at this is the relationship between the body (entity) and shadow (manifest effect). When the body is crooked the shadow is also crooked. If a person's actions are distorted originating from a distorted mind (oneness of body and mind)-shiki shin funi, his results in his life will also take on that distortion in the form of suffering (shadow)-manifested effect. This ultimately means that all suffering that manifest in one's environment(internal and external) is directly related to the individual's mind or the collective mind's of all the people in that environment. This is the principle of Esho funi, the oneness of life (body) and its environment (shadow).

In the first volume of the Lotus Sutra it states, "The true aspect of all phenomena can only be understood and shared between Buddhas." The Daishonin explains this to mean in, <u>The Kalpa of Decrease</u>, "In the phase "consistency from beginning to end," "beginning" indicates the root of evil and the root of good, while "end" indicates the outcome of evil and the outcome of good. One who is thoroughly awakened to the nature of good and evil from their roots to their branches and leaves is called a Buddha." [16]

The illusion that most people follow is to try to make the shadow stand up by focusing on it externally (trying to manipulate the environment and other people). The source of the shadow is from the self (spiritual disorder from

---

[16] (The Gosho Translation Committee, 92)

within); the inherent cause (karma) that produces the manifest effect in the environment. This is the most difficult illusion for a common mortal to perceive.

The 3 poisons of the mind (greed, anger and stupidity) are said to manifest as the conditions of famine, war and pestilence. So, this shows how important and practical it is to be responsible for purifying one's heart and mind through the practice of Buddhism (Hendoku Iyaku- Changing poison into medicine), which extinguishes the source of all the sufferings, which originate from within each and every individual. This sheds light on the fact that the information present in the higher technologies of the day (3rd circuit) provide very little solution to the multiple problems that exist in life today. True Buddhism can clarify the complete source, the inherent cause of our minds (karma) and ignorance. Bodhisattva Nagarjuna explained the Lotus Sutra's superior status among the Buddhas teachings as follows, "The Lotus Sutra is like a great physician who changes poison into medicine."[17] The Daishonin adds to this saying, " This means that a physician of lesser skill can cure ordinary illness with medicine, while a great physician (Lotus Sutra) can cure even grave illness with virulent poison (Earthly desires)."[18]

In the above example, it cannot be clearly seen how the person's past actions created the karma (skin sensitive to excessive sun light) to be at risk for developing skin cancer. But, as you probe into the depths of life and karmic reward you will find that all of reality as experience by each and every being is consistent with one's mind (inherent cause) from the infinite past. The Daishonin

---

[17] (The Gosho Translation Committee, 92)
[18] (The Gosho Translation Committee, 92)

also states in Letter from Sado, "Even more so are past slanders of the Law, which stain the depth of one's heart. A sutra states that both the crow's blackness and the heron's whiteness are actually the deep stains of their past karma."[19] This is consistent with the principle of the oneness of mind and body (shikishi funi) as an individual relates to all phenomenal expressions of life, as it is manifest from moment to moment. There are no mistakes in the perfect manifestation of the law of cause and effect, only suffering as one's mind moves away (illusions or ignorance) from the awareness of this constant truth in life.

It may be necessary to give more illustration of how all of this falls together. Let's say someone was angry at you (the world of anger within another sentient being). So, in order to get even with you they decide to destroy your home while you are at work (inherent cause not yet manifest or potentially to happen in your life-karma). After 5 hours at work you return home to see all of your (karmic relationship) valuables destroyed and covered with messages of hate (external cause). Your reaction to this is a change in life experience, which may have been rapture after receiving a phone call from a beautiful woman at work; you had met in a bar 3 weeks earlier, whom you thought would never call you. She was interested in you and planned to meet you at your home 9p.m. that night. The power of this discovery in your home (external cause) was greater than the power of the condition of rapture you arrived home with, and this influenced your condition to change to that of anger (latent effect). The manifested effect is the expression on your face, the physiological changes in

---

[19] (The Gosho Translation Committee, 92)

your body and the action you take (creation of new karma) in response to this event.

This example displays the interrelatedness between the 3 realms of the 1.individual (entity composed of the 5 components of life; form, perception, conception, volition and consciousness), 2.the realm of other sentient beings- people and 3.the environment.

As the dynamic aspects of each of the 10 worlds, 10 factors and the 3 realms interplay with each other, these realities intermingle to give life the objective appearance it has as it manifest in each and every phenomenon (shoho jisso). Every person sees life exactly the way they see it as true (subjective truth or belief), whether in the condition of hell, rapture or learning. Each experience is unique to that individual's condition of life and perceptions relative to that condition. Nichiren Daishonin states in Reply to Soya Nyudo, "Each character of this Lotus sutra is without exception a living Buddha of supreme enlightenment, but we ordinary people, viewing the sutra with the eyes of common mortals, see it as a mere succession of characters. Hungry spirits perceive the Ganges River as fire, human beings perceive it as water, and heavenly beings perceive it as amrita."[20] (Amrita is the Sanskrit word for ambrosia.) The same objective reality is seen a different way by each individual based on their life condition (one of the 10 worlds) and their inherent cause (karma). For a person to experience happiness in any environment (external cause), he must purify his inherent cause (8th consciousness- alaya) so that there is no potential negative effect (manifest effect) to be experienced (shadow or latent effect). This is the

---

[20] (The Gosho Translation Committee, 92)

nature of a Buddha's life (free of impurities or negative cause). So, regardless of what conditions manifesting in the environment (external cause) of a Buddha, he or she has no reason to experience negativity (latent effect) from the expressions of the phenomenal world (shoho jisso). When a person's 8th consciousness is clear, the pure influence of the 9th consciousness, the Buddha nature can shine through unobstructed to all expressions of one's life (7th consciousness, 6th consciousness (conscious mind) and down through all the 5 senses with complete pure perception and clarity). This is why the Buddha is known as the awakened one, and has the all encompassing wisdom of reality. It is because his view of life is unobstructed from within.

According to the teachings of Buddhism there are 6 causes of illness;

1. Disharmony of the four elements: earth, water, fire and wind.
2. Immoderate eating and drinking.
3. Poor posture.
4. An attack by demons from without (i.e. viruses and bacteria); demons are considered negative functions or influences which deprive people of happiness or obstruct their correct judgment.
5. The work of devils from within.
6. The effects of karma.

The Nirvana Sutra states, "By serving the three treasures, one can avoid falling into hell in the next life, but will instead suffer afflictions of the head, eyes or back in this one."[21] The Maka Shikan also states, "illness occurs when evil

---

[21] (The Gosho Translation Committee, 92)

karma is about to be dissipated."[22] From this understanding it becomes clear that the appearance of illness represents a process of spiritual awakening and transformation towards a higher state of being. Thus it becomes a means of completing one's path towards spiritual wellbeing.

This clarifies that true complete healing is not the absence of the disease process per se, but is a condition of complete spiritual strength that is derived from the awakening of our core fundamental Buddha nature residing in the amala-consciousness. In this state of life our powerful spirit becomes the source of our true life in the mist of all life experiences that we perceive as being either good or bad as a common mortal. The only true problem that exists for the individual in the mist of his daily conditions is that he is weak spiritually. To illustrate, if a baby was to try to lift a chair he would injure himself in the process. However, an adult can easily move the chair without difficulty. Our daily life problems are similar to this situation. Because we do not possess spiritual strength derived from the core of our being, we find ourselves being defeated by the numerous difficulties that present themselves in daily life.

A person who is awakened to his own Buddha nature can overcome any difficulty in life. We human beings believe that true healing and happiness is the absence of disease and problems. However, when we look at the example of the function of our immune system, we can see how strength is the inherent cause that directs us towards a complete and truly indestructible state of well-being and true happiness. If two people were to contract the same illness, one person

---

[22] (The Gosho Translation Committee, 92)

may overcome the sickness while the other may pass away. The key difference between these two individuals is only their relative strength.

The immune system of both individuals is made from the inherent ability to overcome the attack of viruses and bacteria. In a strange paradox it is the exposure to and resistance established from those very bacteria that gives an individual the ability to overcome the condition produced by those agents. This is the inherent development of strength that is acquired to survive a full blown exposure to the disease.

The above process is the same holographic ally throughout a person's life. It is the ability to acquire internal spiritual strength to overcome the natural flow of problems/ life resistance that is necessary to becoming a truly healthy and happy person. The human perception of life's phenomena is most often dualistic in nature. To experience temperature for example, one would have a preference to the conditions being either too hot or cold. Temperature within itself is a neutral phenomena, non dualistic in nature. We only consider things based on how we feel about our own experience with the phenomena, being our subjective conditioning to the circumstance or situation. The subjective realm or experience we have is the product of many past experiences that cause us to draw conclusions and perceptions of what it is we should do next. Habits and instincts are shaped from the reflections of our experience outlined within the 7th (mano) and 8th (alaya) consciousness.

Chapter 3

Nichiren Daishonin's Teachings

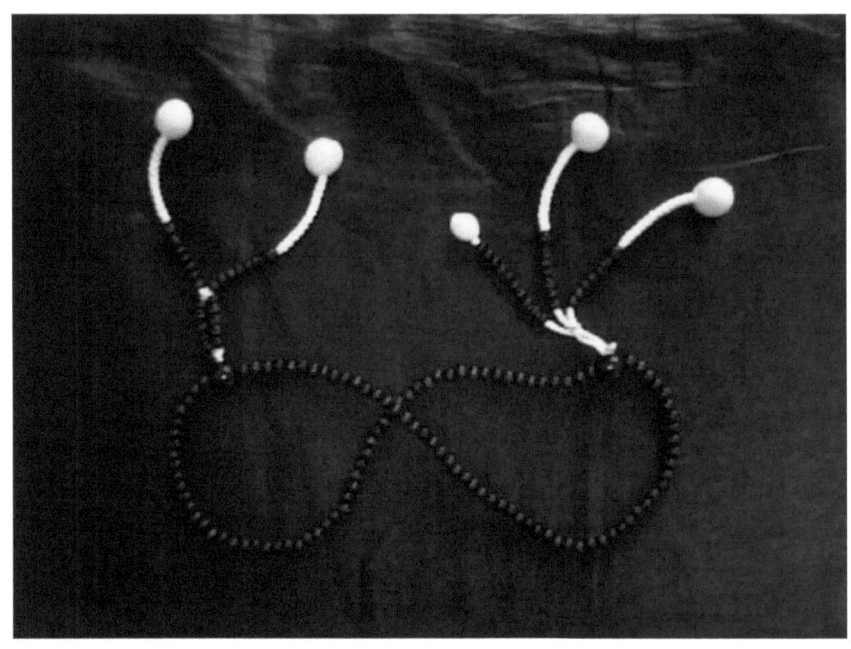

Juzu Beads of Nichiren Shoshu

Nichiren Daishonin integrated the principle of the 108 desires into his teaching as a means to allow the practitioners of True Buddhism to accumulate the benefits of attaining Buddhahood in their daily practice of chanting the Daimoku (Nam Myoho Renge Kyo) and recitation of the Lotus Sutra (Gongyo).

The following describes why Nichiren Shoshu Buddhist uses the prayer beads known as Juzu. The significance of the 108 primary beads completes the relationship between those things or objects we perceive through our senses and the response we have to these phenomena known as desires. The number 108 can be found by the following formula:

6 senses of Eyes, ears, nose, mouth, skin and the mind (perception)

X 3 aspects of time (past, present, and future)

= 18

X 2 characteristics of one's heart (pure or impure). Good or evil based on one's karma.

= 36

X 3 preferences a person may (like, dislike or be indifferent) have to something he perceives through the 6 senses.

= 108 potential conditions of one's desires.

As one practices True Buddhism his heart and desires become pure by purifying the 6 sense organs. Nichiren Daishonin states, "Regard purification of the 6 sense organs as benefit. I, Nichiren and my disciples can receive this benefit by chanting Nam Myoho Renge Kyo."[23] By this process one develops the correct perception through the action of the Daimoku (one meaning of Daimoku is concentration- Dai and eyes or vision- moku), focusing one's eyes or perception on the objective truths of life (Gohonzon) shoho jisso. Nam (subjective mind and body) – the 6 senses or the 5 components used to practice- fusion to Myoho Renge Kyo , which is everything we experience as a common mortal viewed from

---

[23] (The Gosho Translation Committee, 92)

impurity in the 9 worlds, and viewed from purity as a Buddha 10th world.

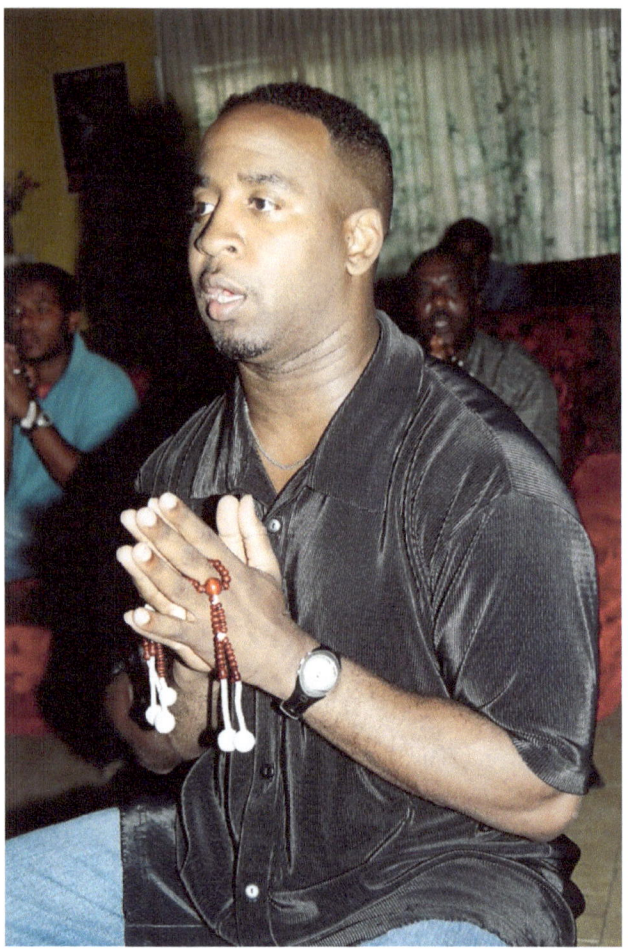

Prayer posture with Juzu Beads over heart

Palms together over the heart symbolize the fusion of Kyo and Chi. Objective truth (Law) and subjective wisdom (faith in the Gohonzon) Buddha as self. The 2 large beads at each end are the parent beads that symbolize this, being the father on the left (Myo) - the Law and the mother on the right (Ho) - wisdom of the Buddha. Our 10 fingers together symbolize the mutual possession of the 10 worlds, which fuse together and manifest simultaneously in the life of a Buddha. As opposed to a common mortal who manifest one world at a time (i.e.

Hell, anger, rapture, learning etc.) On the Gohonzon (True object of Worship) all 10 worlds are represented for this reason all at once.

The 4 smaller beads are the 4 leaders of the Bodhisatvas. Covering the 4 Bodhisatvas and the 108 beads representing desires with our hands in prayer symbolize the principle – Bonno soku Bodai, which is portrayed as the deity Aizen on the middle left side of the Gohonzon. This can mean earthly desires transform into enlightenment. Aizen is often seen with 6 arms which serve as a means of encouraging the believer by offering benefits (desires) to support one's path of faith.

(Rev. Yoshida distributes Juzu to Ethiopian believers in Addis Ababa)

The Fugen sutra states, "You do not need to extinguish your earthly desires and throw away your 5 desires. Only when you are able to purify your senses, will your offenses from your past lives disappear."[24]

The long tassels mean our chanting is spreading to the world- Kosen Rufu. The 3 groups of 10 beads equal 3000 realms in a single moment of life. The 5 balls and the pot shaded beads keep our benefits. The Nichiren Shoshu Priests have 4 long extended balls (tassels) which symbolize their status as teachers to share their benefit (photo above). The beads receive the eye opening ceremony in front of the Dai Gohonzon by the High Priest of Nichiren Shoshu, so that they become the entity (body and mind) of the Buddha in our life to practice to the Gohonzon.

---

[24] (The Gosho Translation Committee, 92)

Imbalances in the human energy field are intermediary to the process of awakening to one's Buddha nature, just as one's ability to develop physical and mental abilities resides in an entirely different area in life. To be able to facilitate healing one needs to encounter a positive influence. This can be a person who has develop a certain level of attributes that distinctively allow him or her to exert influence on those of lesser capacity in a particular aspect of life, be it spiritually, mentally or energetically in a healing state. These people have always been those who have helped humanity move up the scale of evolution.

Nichiren Daishonin is the person with the capacity (power) to lead all living being to complete and true happiness, Buddhahood. He has created the unique way for all people to do this by establishing the Ho Honzon. An object of influence or worship needed to activate our inherent Buddha nature which is a passive Buddha nature, as opposed to the active Buddha nature that is possessed by this true object of worship known as the Dai Gohonzon. The Daishonin, himself was considered the Nin Honzon, the object of worship or influence as a person capable of leading others to Buddhahood as the direct teacher (positive influence). Ho can be translated to mean Law or objective truth inherent in life and Nin translates as the person or Buddha.

Buddhism can be seen as a science of life that gives objective precise details to all of life's phenomena and the Human experience. To establish the profound truth of Buddhism, it will be beneficial to note that Buddhism as taught by the Great Sage Nichiren Daishonin is not to be transmitted in any way that deviates from the precise objectivity of his original words or meaning, which unfortunately must be translated from Japanese to other languages. Just as precise detail is needed when an airplane manufacturer translates vital equipment details from one language to another, the error of discrepancy is exceedingly hazardous in Buddhism within a person's spiritual life and experiences. With any great source of power, respect and wisdom are always increasingly necessary for people to derive benefit from the source. There are many complex and profound principles in Buddhism that can take many years to understand, which can be very frustrating to an individual who seeks the teachings of Buddhism to find meaning and happiness in their life. For the reader to know how a True Buddhist arrives at validating what is true, in Buddhism the three proofs are used, which can clarify any religious or scientific finding.

The three proofs consist of documentary proof, theoretical proof and actual proof (observable fact). Nichiren Daishonin elaborated on this when he stated in the writing, <u>Three Tripitaka Masters Pray for Rain</u>, "In judging the relative merit of Buddhist doctrines, I, Nichiren, believe that the best standards are those of reason (theory) and documentary proof. And even more valuable than reason and documentary proof is the proof of actual fact."[25] To illustrate this we can look back in time to a hypothetical situation 200 years ago involving several farmers. In this meeting of friends, one of the farmers exclaims that it's possible to travel 80 miles per hour. The other farmers fall off their seats laughing at this statement. At this point, the one farmer begins to explain his

---

[25] (The Gosho Translation Committee, 92)

idea using the principles he has read out of the current science books of his time. He uses a chalk board to draw the conclusions he has arrived at, piecing the fundamental concepts of chemistry and mechanical physics together to try to prove his point. However, despite his elaborate presentation on the chalkboard, his points have fallen on deaf ears. At this point he has established documentary and theoretical proof. Since this farmer's progressive thinking is far beyond his close associates he ventures off to prove his belief in travel at 80 miles per hour by spending the next several months crystallizing his thoughts and concepts into what finally takes the shape of the world's first automobile. After several months of being absent, the farmer reappears with his new invention, and asks his friends to take a seat inside.

The farmer then proceeds to drive himself and his friends to the incredible speed of 80 miles per hour and at this point establishes the most important and final proof; actual proof. It is very important to note that there is a great deference between what an individual believes and what that individual knows. Many belief systems require effort for them to maintain a significant influence over their adherents behavior relative to the acts of devotion, because the faith in those systems of understanding or religion have no clear observable facts or experience to move beyond the scope of faith. On the other hand, knowing something is relative to a clear and direct experience for that individual minus projections and images. To illustrate, if a person ate Italian food he has had the direct knowledge of its' taste and characteristic flavors, as opposed to an individual who has just heard about the nature of its taste from someone else.

In religion, people fall into belief for many different reasons or influences. The primary reasons are usually social and based on feelings and emotions. A family's religious background has the heaviest influence on a person's foundation for a particular belief. The primary motive for most western beliefs is fear of evil and suffering or the punishment of hell. The foundation of Buddhism begins with the principle of cause and effect. Some people with a Christian background have some understanding of this concept when they say, "What goes around comes around". However, when you look at this in a practical daily life way, the view of the Christian becomes incomplete. For example, if three different people sinned against Christian views; Hitler killing 6 million people, a man who steals for a living and a atheist, all these people would be destine for eternal hell. This seems like it would make since, but there is one problem. If relatively different crimes were committed by various people, society punishes them all differently. The punishment for killing is completely different than that of stealing and speeding in a car. To look at it from another view, I think it would be very appropriate for the inhabitancy of hell to really show gratitude towards someone like Hitler for his evil actions and to probably impose more torment on those of lesser offenses. This when looked at in a complete view would make very little since out of the completeness of Christian theoretical proof.

(Hokke ji Temple in Accra, Ghana)

The law of cause and effect as defined by Buddhism teaches that every cause one makes comes back to that individual and in some cases the family of that person in a positive or negative form. This can be seen on a practical level when a person looks at his current situation. All the causes a person has made up until 3: 00 p.m., puts him exactly where he stands. And where he is at 8:00 p.m. the following day is entirely base on all the causes he or she makes from that time, until they arrive at 8:00 p.m. the next day. This is simple and yet very profound. This is the beginning to what Buddhism defines as the principle of karma. Since cause and effect is a law, this means that it has always been true and will always be true. This comes from no person or source and is the fundamental difference between Buddhist theoretical proof and Christian theoretical proof. There is one other small question that has to be placed before

both teachings. Where and how do babies get different results from just being born?

For example, some babies are born sick in a country where after only a few days its' mother is killed in civil unrest, in contrast to a baby born into the Kennedy family inheriting millions in wealth and political power from day one. The Buddhist view of life is that everything goes through the continuous cycles of change known as Jo Ju E and Ku. These cycles mean in translation, birth, maturity, decline and death (latency). Cars, planets, atoms, stars, homes, people, cities and all other physical manifestations of matter go through these cycles of birth and death. The law of conservation of energy and matter also supports this premise stating that matter and energy is neither created nor destroyed. It just changes form. As opposed to God created the heavens and the earth, from what? All matter and energy is essentially the same thing that makes up the fabric of life, that which has appearance (physical) and that which has an intrinsic nature –energy (spiritual). In Buddhism this is seen as two expressions of one thing (shiki shin funi) – the oneness of the spiritual and physical aspects of life, which have no beginning or end.

If you superimpose the principle of the natural law of cause and effect over the situation of the two different babies in relation to the natural cycles of matter, you will see that it is a continual truth that you and everyone else is in exactly the situation they have caused themselves to be in at this moment and every moment. If you align this view with the incomplete Christian view, it would just be called fate. The definition of fate according to most people is that it was going to happen anyway or that God destined me for this. This sounds acceptable to most people but it does not shape their true reality. For example, a person may say it was my destiny to become a doctor in this life, but he will never become one if he does not make the causes (school and study) to be a doctor (effect). If this simple analogy is always true in every life situation, how can there be room for a third party (God) to superimpose your results on you (effects). This is a very confusing point for most people of every religion to accept. This ultimately gives them complete responsibility for everything that happens to them.

This may seem kind of harsh but it is the truth. If a baby puts his hand on the stove the fire does not say, "Oh he does not understand, so I will not burn him." In contrast to the rocket scientist that completely understands fire. He will be burned too. This is the strictness of life's functions and human beings only suffer because of ignorance and illusions to the laws that govern the universe. Specifically, the law of cause and effect, for what is suffering other than effects that we don't like to experience. It's just that simple. How do we get those effects? Answer, by making the deluded causes ourselves. This is where the correct religion is very important.

For example, if my religion states that gravity does not work on my side of the street. I am going to act in accordance with that belief. This is usually documented and theoretically stated in this religion's writings. However much I profess faith in this teaching, my results are always going to be demonstrated in my actual experiences with gravity (objective truth). These are the effects I receive in my daily life that is directly related to whether I am going to suffer from broken bones or paralysis. This is a clear example of how one's religious

beliefs cause unpleasant effects in a person's life. Unfortunately for most people

King Togbe Degenu and Nana Asomani founder of NST Ghana

they get coached into believing that the reason for their suffering is that they did not believe hard enough or that God was just testing your faith. If you don't catch yourself at the beginning steps of such a misleading distortion of objective truth, you will live a life of complete suffering, which is shrouded by the illusions of others who have no sound theoretical bases for giving you clarity in your situation. This is the importance of actual proof.

Other religions teach that one's actual proof will be experienced when they die. This seems very ridiculous if you think of working for 60 years in order to get a paycheck at the end of your long years of work. I'm sure no one would work for a company like that. Even if this was true, how would you prove it theoretically or actually to someone else if you were deceased? To add, most

people are afraid to die, yet they work so hard and long to get to heaven. In the time of King James the belief was that when the tower of Babel was constructed heaven was depicted as being above the clouds. So, if a Christian is going to heaven he always refers to going up from the place where he is standing, but this defies the facts that have become clear over time since then. As we all know Christopher Columbus proved to all of Europe that the earth was round. With this amazing discovery he disproved a major concept in the predominant Christian view unknowingly. Then with the discovery of fossil remains of gigantic monsters that roamed the Earth 60 million years ago and oil, we dissolved the entire foundation of the principle of creation that the Bible's documentary proof stands on. The people who die in China would have to go in an entirely different direction than those of us who wanted to go to heaven from the United States. This is very confusing as you can see. It's no wonder that most people are completely confused about most things in life.

This brings us into the foundation of the principle of what enlightenment is. The term Kyo Chi Myogo can be translated to mean the fusion of objective truth with the correct subjective relation to that truth (belief). Objective truth corresponds to the laws that permeate this reality we live in, specifically the law Myoho Renge Kyo. The illustration of gravity can be used to help understand this point. Two hundred years ago the people who lived on the North American continent would probably take 2 or 3 months to walk across the current area known as the United States. This was because they were probably walking or on horse, and had to go across many rivers and mountain ranges. These people probable understood instinctively that the principle of gravity affected them and that it was necessary to climb up and down hills and mountains safely. But, after 100 or more years a person named Sir Isaac Newton developed an understanding of the principle of gravitational law. After which many forms of physical science created the theoretical means for us to develop airplanes. Now at this time it is only a matter of hours for us to get from one side of the United States to the other. This is all possible because we have taken the correct subjective relation to the objective truth, which is the law of gravity. In Buddhism when a person bases his life on the objective law of Myoho Renge Kyo, by devoting himself to its practice Nam (one translation means to devote one's life), he simultaneously creates the correct relationship with all expressions of this complete law that a person who is a Buddha can only understand. As opposed to the laws that the people of the scientific world come to understand like Sir Isaac Newton.

Believing and chanting Nam Myoho Renge Kyo, one creates the same effect in one's life just as proportionally to that of the difference between the people who don't believe in gravity and get broken bones or death from their ignorance and the benefit of those who live in mastery of gravity with airplanes and space shuttle flights. Establishing the correct subjective belief in relation to the absolute objective truth is all that Buddhism is about, nothing more or less. When a person extinguishes his negative causes from his past behavior, which extend into the infinite past and eradicates the illusions of reality that created those bad results from the beginning; he then will take on the attributes of an individual known as a Buddha. This is not so simple because the practice of Buddhism always stems from being responsible for one self and takes on the form of daily effort. Unfortunately, most people still will not grasp the complete concept of how cause and effect works and believe that Buddhism works like magic. Unfortunately, like everything time is required to see actual proof on the deepest level. Just like one week in the weight room will not leave you looking like Lee Haney or Arnold Schwartzenigger. It takes hard practice, study, endurance and most importantly faith in oneself that you will became a Buddha in the future. As a person exhibits the attributes of a Buddha, he or she knows 100% clearly what it is that they must do and not do in life. Most people are under the influence of the weakness of their selfish desires and can only consider what corresponds to their favor. This is an expression of what true dishonesty is in human character, which is typically weak.

Nichiren Daishonin teaches that if there is neither document nor logic one should not believe. If this is so, every person must look at the foundation of everything they believe to arrive at some form of completion in their life. The Daishonin also notes that "even an individual at cross purposes with himself is certain to end in failure."[26] If a person continues to believe various things that when lined up together add up to zero or some negative reality, he or she should have some clue to the source of all their current troubles. The Fugen Sutra states, "The Ocean of impediment of all karmas is produced from one's false imagination." False imagination means the images we derive from what we believe to be true about a curtain course of action we must take to experience happiness. Many of us are disillusioned by what we perceive to be the source of our happiness and conclude latter that our image of the situation was not the

---

[26] (The Gosho Translation Committee, 92)

same as the reality in the outcome. The above is called illusions of thought and desire. Illusions of thought are distorted perceptions of truth. Illusions of desire mean base inclinations such as greed and anger which arise from contact of the five sense organs with their respective objects. These illusions cause one to suffer in the six paths, which are the first six worlds of the Ten Worlds.

Within the fundamental structure of language an individual can come to release themselves from one of the basic webs of delusion by distinguishing the difference between belief and the experience of knowing. For example, an individual expresses belief in something when there is in fact no tangible experience. If one individual where to dine at a particular restaurant, he or she would know (experience) that the food was either bad or good in taste. Relaying their words of their experience to other individuals would create the condition for their belief that the food is either good or bad. The primary individual is in the position of knowing, which is a more superior position than that of belief within the secondary individuals, which have no experience of the foods' taste. Relative to religion, the above is the inherent issue. People have no concrete proof in their lives as it relates to the end product of the focus of their beliefs, actual experience.

(The High Sanctuary of True Buddhism home to the Dai Gohonzon)

Chapter 4

Tools for Healing

The means for healing oneself vary according to one's belief system and exposure culturally. The highest levels of healing may in general be difficult to come by since the level of education and back ground of an individual will provide a difficult obstacle for them to embrace such a profound reality. This would be a large leap of faith for the individual who is unaware of the deeper truths that exist in life, and only feels comfortable following the norms of current day healing modalities. The absence of role relationship with oneself and others is a large aspect of the intrinsic conflict that obstructs any form of productivity within an individual's life.

Role Relationship is the key to absolute productivity and harmony within an individual, group or organization. The roles are divided into Female and Male roles. The male role has 100% Responsibility and 100% Authority in relation to the dynamics of the equation. The Female Role has 0% Responsibility and 0% Authority. To have 100% productivity in relation to the purpose of the relationship overall, this balance of Responsibility and Authority must always be maintained. An example of why this is the case will unfold in the following illustrations.

In a hospital setting we find a doctor, a nurse and a patient who has come for treatment of a particular ailment. Upon admission to the clinic the doctor directs the nurse to tell the patient to remove his clothing, so he can examine him. The doctor in this setting is assuming the Male Role relative to the nurse in this initial transaction. The nurse playing the perfect Female Role to the doctor offers no resistance or objection to his request and follows through with his instructions informing the patient that he must remove his clothes so that he can be examined by the doctor. In the transaction between the nurse and the patient, the nurse now becomes the Male Role taking on the Responsibility conferred to her or him by the doctor in charge. This patient however, objects to removing his clothing at the request of the nurse, subsequently making it impossible for the doctor to eventually provide the examination and services needed for him to resolve his presenting complaint for treating. This patient is unable to play the Female Role, which surrenders all Authority and Responsibility over to the Male Role being the nurse who instructed him. In this scenario it is clearly observable how if the role relationship is not played in accordance with the specific equation giving the male role 100% Responsibility and Authority, the outcome will be little or no productivity. In the above conclusion the result was a contest, which can be seen as two opposing Male Roles trying to maintain some form of Authority and or Responsibility in the transaction, producing a non productive situation. (Fig. 4) Role Relationship is therefore a manifestation of the flow of energy along the path of least resistance.

The Role Relationship also exists within oneself. In this situation the roles are played between the inner spiritual impulse, the mind and the body.

In the morning a man sleeps in bed beyond his normal waking time resisting the impulse to get up to prepare for his daily routine. The spirit within this person has the ambition to do very valuable work for humanity, if it can manage to train and get complete control over the body assigned to its task. However, this individual's mind is very lazy and lacks commitment and concern for others, so it prefers to spend more time enjoying the comforts of the pillow and bed. The physical body is powerless to do anything outside of the volitional constraints of the mind.

In this situation, the individual has not disciplined himself enough to be the most productive individual possible, because he has not surrendered control and authority of his mind and body over to his spirit or higher self. If the role relationship between his spirit, mind and body was complete he would be experiencing the fruits of his productivity in the form of more motivation to carry out the rest of his life with enthusiasm. Here is a relative glimpse at the secret to success in all areas of one's life, which is nothing other than making a habit of doing the things that one does not like to do.

Someone may ask what those things might be. Simply stated, they are the very things that most people dislike doing. For example, the discipline and dedication needed to train as a great athlete, specialist or scholar. The average person usually gives in to his or her base preference during the decision making process in their life, preventing them from making extra ordinary feats or accomplishments a possibility.

This is why it is clearly known that less than 5% of the population is considered to be successful in their activities of choice, be it relationships, careers, health or spiritual objectives. This would conclude that it is unnatural to be successful since following the specific norms of behavior displayed by the average man produce nothing significant. Since success is an unnatural thing relative to the norms of reality, one would likewise have to conclude that the means for obtaining success in any endeavor requires going against what would be the natural behavior of the individual's preference. This ultimately means disregarding what is considered to be the favorite or most desirable path.

Communication is at the heart of all forms of order and disorder that exist between two or more individuals. Communication is the form of transmission between the Male and Female roles. Order exists when truth (Law) is being transmitted from one individual (Male role) to another who receives that input with complete focus (Female role), offering no resistance to that reality as being factual; the realm of faith (consents to male action). Images are not truth and therefore can be the source of disharmony when transmitted or received within a Role Relationship (Fig. 4). Fear, the direct opposite of faith (Negative Syndrome/evaluation) is also a form of resistance (lack of submission); grounded in an illusion created by an image of reality that separates oneself from the objective truth.

CONTEST:

Contestant 1   VS.   Contestant 2

Nonproductive:

ROLE RELATIONSHIP:

Productive:

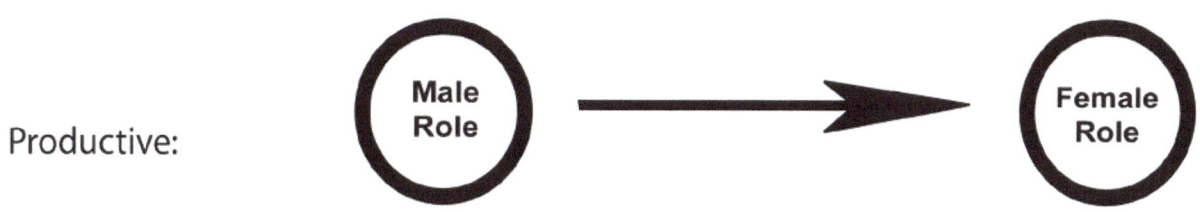

Male Role	Female Role
1. Selects a female role	
2. Initiates action	3. Receives action from male role
	4. Consents to action
5. Accepts her consent	
6. Accepts 100% responsibility	7. Consents with 5 S's
	A. Surrender
	B. Subordination
	C. Subservience
	D. Subjection
	E. Submission
8. Accepts 100% Authority	

Fig. 4

It is very important to note that when there is a lack of communication or contact between individuals, there is a tendency for the creation of images and projections to occur relative to the emotional aspect of the relationship. This can and does produce conflict, because the mind becomes separated from the clarity of the original intent of the relationship. This gives more gravity to the importance of clear continual communication being the foundation of harmony and productivity between two or more individuals. All involved must share this common responsibility.

The Authority that the Male role has is the Law or Principle to which he or she is enlightened. Since principles and Laws are the fabric of the Universe we live in, the reality shaped within the relationship between the Male and Female roles are going to reflect the same profound order that exist within the Universe on a microcosmic scale. This is the universal equation of harmony and productivity in all of Natures' functions and the manifestation of true faith for the Female Role.

Since dis-ease/non productivity is the manifestation of illness within an individual's body, at some level the person has dissolved some form of communication within themself or has never learned to establish it. Pain is usually the last call (communication) for help from the inside. Unconsciousness or the lack consciousness is the absence of a relationship with the Male role/ principle (spirit) to direct the processes of life in a conscious (Female role) divine manor, in the physical plain (matter/body).

To illustrate the power of the above equation relative to communication, let's look at the use of cellular phones as an example. The original concept and use of cellular phones was to aid in the effectiveness in communication in the business world, to increase productivity and efficiency overall. As the concept and convenience of the cellular phone became more popular, many individuals outside the business world have decided to acquire the cellular phone for personal use. Interesting enough a very important phenomenon has occurred relative to the use of these phones among individuals who use them for personal use. It would seem that these individuals who possess these phones acquired them for the same reasons large corporations have, to increased productivity in their relations and communications with others. However, upon close observation these individuals have found themselves moving deeper into disconnection from others and themselves.

When a person receives a call from someone that they do not want to speak to, the phone provides them with the information about who in fact is calling. Internally the person comes in contact with feelings that they do not want to experience or a twisted aspect of expression, which is nothing short of deception of self and others, lies. If the person has a pattern of not being in communication with their inner feelings in relationship to others, this holographic ally represents the dynamics of the dis-ease process in its' evolution towards the physical dimension in the body's health, interpersonal relationships and the environment. Transmission of truth (Laws and Principles) requires internal strength (higher potential energy/ spiritual force) and the responsibility to maintain the order of the universe in one's own personal way (wisdom); from this standpoint the male role has the power, which must be directed towards a Female Role that consents to the 5 S's of surrender, subordination, subservience, subjection and submission. This is the process of faith for the Female Role to obey. Fusion with the male role on a spiritual level is only possible under these conditions. This oneness or fusion between the male and female roles is called the Master-disciple relationship, which is the only means of a disciple/ female to attain Buddhahood (Enlightenment). This is the process or flow within Buddhism that is termed Kechimyaku (Fig. 5), which means the transmission of the life blood inheritance entrusted to only one person by the Buddha, that is a unbroken transfer of spiritual Authority and Responsibility through the specific role relationship between each successive High Priest of Nichiren Shoshu originating with the True Buddha Nichiren Daishonin.

Two Types Of kechimyaku

1. Entity of The law
2. Of Faith

Time	Believers(2)	High Priest Lineage	Believers (2)
1282AD	Alive with High Priest	Nichiren Daishonin's life Equals <Dai Gohonzon> (person & Law) ↓	Living at the time with the High Priest
	←	Nikko Shonin+ Dai Gohonzon	→
1333AD	←	Nichimoku Shonin + Dai Gohonzon	→
	←	↓ Other High Priest ↓	→
1726AD	←	Nichikan Shonin + Dai Gohonzon	→
	←	↓ Other High Priest	→
Now	←	↓ Nichinyo Shonin + Dai Gohonzon	Living at the time with Nichinyo Shonin
	←	Linear Kechimyaku	→ Horizontal Kechimyaku
		1. Hottai no kechimyaku or the entity of the law	2. Shinjin no kechimyaku or kechimyaku of faith
	Believers	High Priest	Believers

Fig. 5

Kechimyaku of Nichiren Shoshu

Within the person who is conscious of the principles and order upon which the universe is established, resides a profound intention to communicate clearly, accurately and completely, so that what resides within their being can come to full expression in the physical world. Lack of clarity in communication would without exception manifest as disorder in the physical realm. This without question points to the fact that a true relationship between two individuals would mean not having an emotional, psychological or financial advantage over the other to create a situation that is manipulated towards one parties own selfish interest. Nichiren Daishonin stated that, "one's enemies will try to deceive you."[27] One's enemies can therefore be seen as any agent or intention against truth disrupting full awareness and consciousness.

Many individuals want to develop themselves spiritually; however the fruits of their efforts many times give them very little evidence of what it is they assumed would be the outcome of that often brief search for a divine experience. People often assume that this shift in reality would expose them to some kind of miraculous powers and insights that they often read about or see in many science fiction books and movies. To note that such powers are indeed an aspect of reality for human beings to experience, what would be the qualifications for the acquisition of such ability? To shed more light on this from the stand point of the principles in the universe (male role); let us look at it in more practical manor. Suppose there is a couple that decides to leave town for the weekend, leaving 4 children at their residence to be looked after by the most responsible in their absence. The most likely scenario would be to leave the oldest child in

---

[27] (The Gosho Translation Committee, 92)

charge of the 3 younger children, giving that child 100% responsibility and authority 100% over the use of finances and the home during the parent's absence. This responsibility and authority given to this child demonstrates the parents trust and confidence placed in this child to act in their best interest relative to their property and inherent value of the children's safety in their absence.

In the above situation, the parents represent the universal laws that exist or principles of the divine and the oldest child represents the spiritual master that has become self actualized relative to the principle or teaching of divine truth that they have mastered and must transmit to others correctly with the same mind.

In short, the oldest child is the male role; however they must play the female role to the parents or the principle which they stand for. The same is true for the spiritual master relative to his relationship to the disciples and the principles (Laws) he serves. In contrast to the above, what do you think would happen if the youngest was given the responsibility for the property and safety of the other children? As you could imagine, the order and valued assets of the parent's would be at high risk for loss. The many years of effort needed to acquire and develop what the family has could be lose due to negligence of an immature child who is not even capable of taking care of their own needs. Money is power, and responsibility is also needed to manage that power or any other virtue that one has acquired. Not knowing the above as it relates to the spiritual is one of the primary grounds for why many individuals cannot find access to the divine relationship with the spiritual laws and principles that exist.

The immaturity and pure negligence that these individuals have relative to their own lives, does not allow them access to the fabric of divine experience which has to be worn in service to the order of the divine and absolute truth. On the spiritual path of development these individuals like all children must seek the instruction of a master who is divinely representing as a female to the core principles that they are in service to.

There is an order of priority that one must follow to support the development of net worth, profit or value in one's life. This takes the form of the 4 P's, which are;

1. Profit- monetary or spiritual gain and development
2. Protection- creating safety and security for what one considers the most valuable attributes of his or her existence; i.e. the three types of treasures: treasure of the body, treasure of the storehouse and the treasure of the heart (see glossary).
3. Pride- the establishment of one's self worth relative to non egotistical perspectives
4. Pleasure- the enjoyment of life

If one is to create a net value from the activities of his or her life, the priority of his daily activities should follow the above order of importance.

To profit or benefit in life is an underlying theme in the life of most people, however there is no rhyme to the reason. Looking at the activities of daily life, people are motivated by one of the 4 P's in a relatively different order than is outlined above.

Pleasure may well be the primary motive behind the activities of most individuals from morning to evening. Profiting monetarily or spiritually would probably place last on the list of priorities listed, since most people are programmed to be the perfect consumer.

Wisdom is the ability to create the most favorable outcome in a situation relative to the variables that are presented to that individual. In one given situation, three individuals are given $1.00 with which to use for whatever they wish. Each person relative to their perception of reality and motivation will have a different experience upon receiving the money. The first individual makes the decision to spend the dollar, the second person is motivated to save their dollar and the third person was able to transform the dollar into 20 dollars. Each person's experience or concluding result was based upon their inherent wisdom as it applied to the understanding of how reality works in reference to creating the most profitable conclusion to what had been presented to them.

In a different perspective each person experiences life relative to their overall state of consciousness and wisdom of the underlying laws that govern a particular phenomena or life experience. To master one's life it is necessary to be well versed in the objective truths that exist eternally throughout time and space. This is nothing other than the fusion between objective reality (Laws) and wisdom (subjective comprehension of truth) exhibited in ones' behavior.

The universe or the environment is composed of the 5 elements that are contained in the human body, which we depend on for survival. Our mastery or harmonious balance in relationship to these elements which are; earth, water, fire, wind and spirit (non-substantiality) is based entirely on our belief systems and intentionality in life.

In the not so distant past people use to believe that fire was evil, due to their negative experiences with it. For example fire was the cause of great suffering if crops, homes and domestic animals were destroyed by it during blazes started by lightening. From this type of experience people imposed a negative image or devil concept to the element of fire. However, today we use this same fire to heat our homes in the middle of a winter storm to protect us from freezing to death. It is also used to cook our foods and light the darkness just to name a few examples.

From the above illustration it can be seen that fire is a relatively neutral phenomena in the non dualistic nature of the universe. However, our experience with it is relative to our state of consciousness and wisdom to use it effectively to support our existence. All five elements reflect this same truth universally, including the function of our spirit, the most profound of the five to comprehend.

The foundation of how healing works to clear the issues individuals have in relation to the first four circuits begins with connecting to the level of feelings, the heart space. Making deep contact with the issues and images held by each individual creates the relationship for neurological-evolution to begin. As out lined before, the majority of people try to avoid feeling the pain that is held within their system, which retards their advancement.

Using a comprehensive healing plan that includes the use of hands on healing techniques, holistic and western medical doctors, herbalist, psychological counselors, physical and colon therapists sets a solid foundation of support to move the individual into neurological evolution, and out of physical and psychological dis-ease. Knowledge of the circuits and how they work is the primary key to the overall progression and outcome of the healing plan. The healing team (1st phase of the Universal family) should be providing a strong sense of concern and heart level contact with the individual to support this process. However, it can be that some individuals may not need such an extreme level of support, if they have a strong intention and some awareness of this process of self healing and evolution. An individual that has cleared his circuits can affect others through "morphic resonance."

Providing the individual with information about their health as it relates to diet and environment is necessary for supporting spontaneous evolution through the circuits. Information about spiritual laws and principles completes the adult phase of the 3rd circuit, allowing the individual to over ride previous misconceptions about reality. This has to be done in combination with the healing work, to allow the current life issues and images to come to the level of consciousness and integrate with the healthy adult ego. Kyo chi myogo is the absolute completion of the 3rd circuit and spontaneously brings the individual into their true mind of life via the 4th circuit (heart space), which is a state of intrinsically perfect wisdom grounded within the purified human heart (9th consciousness). When an individual reaches the limitations of their current belief system, this is the opportunity to introduce them to the relationship with the Law of cause and effect within Buddhist practice and study.

This is done by them chanting Nam Myoho Renge Kyo and studying the principle teachings established by a sage enlightened to this Law. Kyo means objective truth (teachings) or the universal law (the Buddha's property of the Law) that permeates reality, cause and effect (karma or Renge). Chi means subjective wisdom (mind that perceives the truth of reality- the Buddha's property of wisdom) or the correct relationship to the objective law as depicted in one's behavior (the Buddha's property of action). Myogo means fusion, which translates as the correct spiritual and physical behavior in relationship to the objective law that governs reality eliminating the fundamental source of all suffering, which originates from the breach of its principles (negative karma). This state of life activates the inherent Buddha Nature, which resides at the level of the 9th consciousness (amala- consciousness). The words amala-vijnana are Sanskrit words meaning pure (amala) discernment (vijnana). This is the state of 100% brain function governed by the influence of the 8th circuit, which is being at one with the source, defined as a condition beyond comprehension. From the four dimensional healing model, this relates to the verbal cause (chanting Nam Myoho Renge Kyo) to connect to one's core essence. The energy field becomes balanced equally in its aspects of reason, will and emotion in this state. When and if an individual is open to the above, the teachings of Nichiren Shoshu work to complete or initiate the third and fourth circuit healing process. If the individual currently practices Nichiren Daishonin's Buddhism they are directed to deepen their study of Buddhism.

These 3 aspects of reason, will and emotion within the auric field directly correspond to the instructions given by the enlightened sage Nichiren Daishonin for opening (Myo) the inherent Buddha nature through faith (emotion), practice (will) and study (reason). When all of the chakras are open in relation to the strong intension (hara) to live in truth (kyochi myogo), this is what opens the individual's life to complete health and healing from within (fig.6). It is important to note that the regenerative capacity to re-grow organs and tissue in the body can only be activated with the higher frequencies of brain function residing in the frontal lobes of the brain (7th circuit).

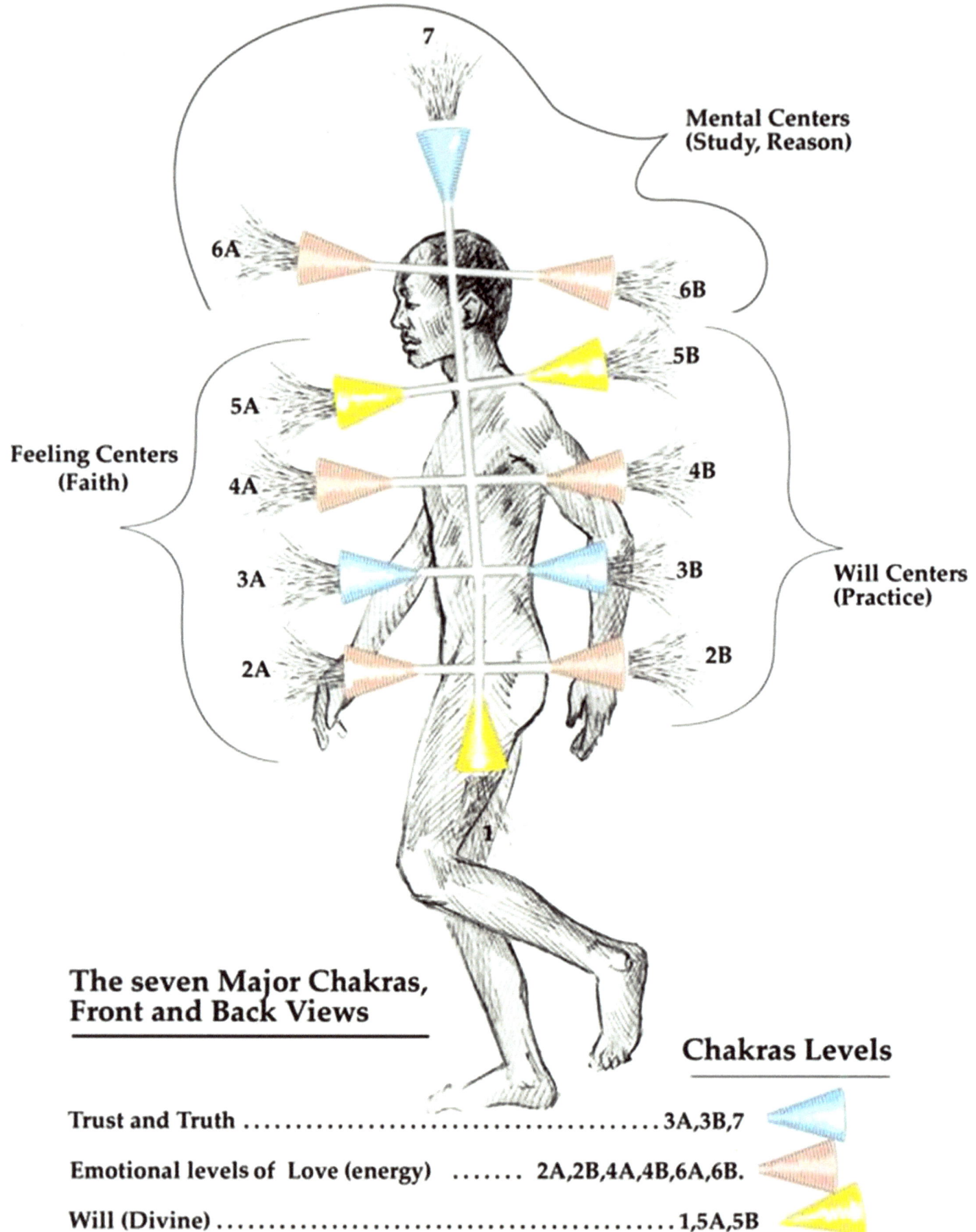

Fig.6

Chakra Diagram of Human Body

Chakras and the Body Areas they Nourish

*Chakra 1- lower part of body, adrenals and tailbone

*Chakra 2- lower pelvis, sex organs, and immune system

*Chakra 3- solar plexus area, stomach, spleen, liver, pancreas and kidneys

*Chakra 4- heart area, circulatory system

*Chakra 5- throat, lungs and ears

*Chakra 6- eyes, head and lower brain

*Chakra 7- upper brain and eyes

Through the healing techniques outlined for progression through the first 4 circuits of the brain, the healer has the capacity to guide the individual through the initiation phases of frontal lobe awakening, by completing the disruptions within the 1st four circuits.

It is interesting to note that the Buddha warns that if you slander the Universal Law (Buddhism), your head will be split in 7 pieces. This can be translated as a person who suffers from mental illness. From the view of completion of the 7 circuits, we all are suffering from mental illness related to incomplete brain function. Hence, we are not in complete reality because of this lack of experiencing all of who we can be. The analogy is like that of a person who has a paralyzed arm with the exception of use of his index finger. By never experiencing or using the complete brain, we have constructed a life based on the incompletion of the true self physiologically, mentally and spiritually.

By looking at the figure illustrating the chakra centers, it can be seen that there is a synergistic relationship between the will and feeling centers. With further observation it can be correlated that when one puts themselves into practical action (will), it relates to some type of faith (emotion) as being the energetic motivation to move forward on the object or idea that may or may not be perceived through the mental centers in the head. This fundamentally equals to action being the death of fear and the birth of faith; faith and fear being direct opposites. When one is preoccupied with problems the will centers begin to respond (open or close) relative to the cognitive processing (mental centers) ability to map out a solution based on a clear perception of reality (truth), pure faith or fear opening or closing the will centers; creating a course of action or lack of it (depression).

By chanting Nam Myoho Renge Kyo the individual will holographic ally transform their environment into a purer condition by purifying his 6 senses(5 senses and the conscious mind) and activating the inherent wisdom(reason) and actions(will) needed to establish the correct path to fulfill their spiritual longing in this and all future lifetimes. Faith (emotion) is what is needed for the person to completely heal on all levels; however this faith must be based on the objective truths of life (reality). It is at the level of relationship where all illness occurs. Likewise it is through the relationship with a healer or person of positive influence that the individual begins their path back to truth, through faith in relationship to others. The relationship with the Gohonzon, which is the manifestation of the fusion of the Person (Buddha) and the Law (Myoho) is the exception to the above kind of relationships. However, it is the difficulties on the emotional level and the fundamental fears within each of the 5 character structures that require faith to transcend.

Opening circuits 1 through 7 equals 100% of brain function and is the full experience of love, which is everything or reality (Kyo chi myogo). One recognizes and experiences themselves and the Universe as the same thing. This is the complete and wholesome state of an individual, which is the divine right and creative expression inherent within each individual human-being. In Hermeticism, the above is called transcending oneself. Before transcendence, each individual is in effect acting under the influence of the "collective soul", described by Jung as "the collective unconscious".[28] In this type of limited morphic resonance, the individual is directed by an invisible force that manages each species of the animal kingdom in relation to reproduction, seasonal migration, territorial demarcation, etc. The power to transform results from the profound understanding of the laws of nature, which are also harnessed in conjunction with hands on healing techniques used in the Barbara Brennan and Frequencies of Brilliance healing modalities.

The Universal Family is the product of individuals that have moved into truth and love by an association with an individual that can translate these realities into human behavior. This is the role of a True Master in life and the profound attributes of a Buddha possessing the spiritual strength and wisdom to lead others. Nichiren Daishonin states in his writing, <u>The Selection Of The Time</u>, "A tick that attaches itself to the tail of a ch'i-lin can race a thousand ri in one day, and a worthless mortal who accompanies a wheel-turning king can

---

[28] (Baines, 1993)

circle in an instant about the four continents of the world." [29] This means that of one's own power we can accomplish very little relative to our poor spiritual condition, however when we associate ourselves with the proper spiritual influence we can effectively transform under the divine principle of the correct relationship with a spiritual leader, which maybe a Buddha or his designated representative.

Love is nature and is also the powerful energy transformed into the physical dimension through the human heart with unlimited wisdom. This love has two sides to it; one born of darkness, called Corrupt Love (fundamental darkness), and another born of light, called Divine Love (Buddha Nature). Corrupt Love is found in a humanity that is locked in the first 3 circuits of brain function. The contrasting concepts of corrupt and divine are simply related to the divine as the natural state and the corrupt as the unnatural, or, the natural corrupted and perverted state.[30]

Humanity is in need of a divine plan back to order from within. Healing the dysfunctions from the perspective of the 7circuits is universal to all people and cultures. The Buddha states that the means to gain entrance to Buddhahood is only through faith. Without faith one only remains at best in the level of Rational Realist (3rd circuit) or falls below into the realm of the Negative Syndrome (fear, hate and evil) or the Evil Paths of the Ten Worlds (Hell, Hunger, Animality and Anger). Relative to the 7 circuits, faith means to

---

[29] (The Gosho Translation Committee, 92)
[30] (Baines, 1993)

transcend the first 3 circuits with an open heart (perfect Female Role) to enter the awareness of the 5th, 6th and 7th circuits.

In human reality, chaos and disorder are present with much greater effect than the power of an ordered structure. For this reason it is essential that the knowledge of the 7 circuits of brain function become noted as a precursor for the development of the true human family. John Baines states that, "men and women separately are only halves of a whole; an incomplete reality of one total truth."[31] It is this integral structure which lovers unconsciously try to achieve. Because of incomplete use of 100% brain function, mankind can only simulate love and that is why love for man, is confusing, sensual, deceptive and soul-killing. Man's ability to love is contaminated with the void of untruths and illusions, which have their foundations in incomplete consciousness, as it relates to limited brain function. Only those who use their intelligence properly can aspire to an awareness of Divine Love.[32]

Those who are guided by base and selfish motives cannot imagine the existence of a higher love. They are content with the simple mating habits of animals. Higher love is achieved through conscious awareness, communication between the purified spirit, mind and body (role relationship). This is the foundation of the Universal Family. As an individual heals them self through the maturation of the brain circuits, they begin to re- orient their value system towards spiritually/ consciousness based awareness, that includes higher principles of the heart as described by the Buddha as the treasure of the heart.

---

[31] (Baines, 1993)
[32] (Baines, 1993)

The final objective of the Buddha's life is the global realization of this deep spiritual awareness of the heart based on the opening of the inherent Buddha nature within each individual, which has been called Kosen Rufu.

Divine Love satisfies the body, mind and spirit. All people who operate from purely instinctual contexts (1st circuit) are excluded from the possibility of attaining true love, 100% brain function. The key to love is transcendence of the baser side of Nature.[33]

Corrupt Love leads invariably to psychological and spiritual self-destruction. The dissolution submits the individual to the raw force of Nature (Kyo), which over the course of time gradually absorbs the person in its stronger principles until they begin to lose their higher faculties and begin to exhibit a solidification of their bestial side, the first 3 circuits. John Baines adds that, "a man who might possess exquisite qualities becomes a boor and a caricature of what he once was, and a woman, delicate, lovely and refined, gradually becomes hard and vulgar. These changes are not necessarily the result of aging, but of the rupture of natural principles."[34]

In light of the above, healing the incomplete circuits of brain function holographic ally to sets the foundation for healing the individual and the universal family, that is comprised of psychologically and spiritually evolved individuals of each gender. Every individual has an inherent longing that can only be found within the universal human family.

---

[33] (Baines, 1993)
[34] (Baines, 1993)

An individual can not realize his or her full potential without completing each of the 7 circuits. A healer and each individual can set the foundation for healing the universal human family through understanding the function and nature of the 7 circuits. When this insight has been established, it can be clearly seen that all dysfunctions within society and human culture have their origins within the misunderstanding and ignorance of the 7 circuits of brain function. Healing the first 4 circuits becomes the foundation of health and well-being within all people. Overall, a person is not fulfilled as a human being until they have completed the true relationship to family and self.

Chapter 5

The Subjective Realm

The human experience is as diverse as there are individuals to live it. One phenomenon can be experienced or seen in a multitude of different ways. Because of the human's emotional nature, reality is always seen in a dualistic manor. For example, if one were to ask people from different racial groups their perspective of what the United States was, you would find quite a different answer from each one of these individuals relative to what has happened to them personally or within a historical perspective. The Native American would consider the United States a place of great deception and suffering relative to their ancestral experience over the past 300 years and their current life in the reservation system. The African American would paint his or her image of the United States as being full of incarceration, drug infested communities, racism, discrimination and personal struggle for equality across the board.

A Caucasian working on Wall Street with a net income of over $100,000 per month would describe the United States as a great place full of opportunities and the American dream. His life experience would include the many luxuries of the life style reflecting his spending power and respect given to him in association with his wealth and charisma. As you can see, the possibilities of what each person would say the United States is entirely subjective in nature.

Each of the 275 million inhabitances would put their particular spin on what they would define it to be.

In contrast to the above, the United States has an objective aspect which is beyond the subjective experience. We all can agree that it has 50 states, and that it has a west coast and a east coast, which are out lined by the Atlantic and Pacific Oceans. There are geographic distinction such as the locations of cities, rivers and mountain ranges relative to each other. Objectively these are all the things that make up aspects of what the United States is to experience.

Diagram of Brain:

1/10 Conscious Mind

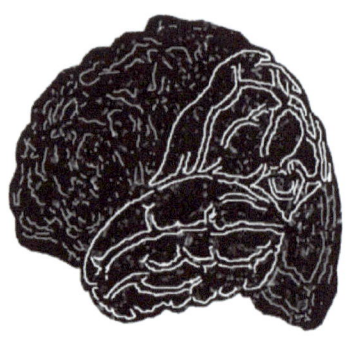 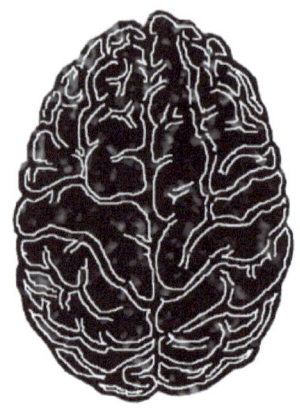

9/10 Subconscious Mind

Functions of the Conscious and Subconscious

The Conscious:
1. Administrative function
2. Has a value system
3. Regulates entire system
4. Has a protective function
5. Has limitations of time and/or space
6. Knows right from wrong

The Subconscious:
1. Has all memory functions
2. Has computers
3. Is the "machine" which builds your personality
4. Has no limitations of time and/or space
5. Like a baby…it believes everything
6. All inputs are additive

Laws:

1. You have only one thought at a time
2. You have complete control of your thoughts (authority and personality)
3. Your personality is the sum total of all the images that you have ever had from birth
4. Anything that enters the conscious mind is recorded in the subconscious mind
5. Time X intensity = POWER OF THE THOUGHT

Whenever you cultivate a thought, remember it will trace, with telling touch, in picture form, its story on your face. Whenever you cultivate a thought, remember it will be a force throughout the universe for all eternity.

Fig.7

Functions of the Brain

Emotions are the most powerful influence illustrating the human experience. The prison systems are full of individuals who are the byproduct of deep emotional disturbances originating in the early developmental stages of life, as illustrated within the five character structures and first 3 brain circuits. The emotional trauma experienced early in life shapes the foundation of the continual cycles of maladaptive behaviors and social stresses experienced by most adults. One may often encounter individuals who continually lament or recycle long ago childhood experiences on a daily basis, as if these events happened only days ago. These facts about human tendencies should clue the individual into how profoundly strong the influences of the heart are to shaping the outcome of an individual's existence. Trust is a major barrier confronting possibilities of opening up these darkened areas of experience.

The brain can be further divided into conscious and subconscious functions, which govern all aspects of the body's processes and actions. When an individual feels a specific emotion the brain produces a chemical environment in the body that can range between acidic and alkaline pH, producing conditions promoting poor or excellent health. If a person continuously lives their life within a specific range of experiences that are internalizes as negative emotions, a chronic state of events will be generated, within the cell chemistry of the body and social environment surrounding this individual. The negative syndrome is the subjective experience ranging between constructive criticism and total apathy. Living a life in the negative syndrome creates the following:

1. A negative body chemistry, resulting in shortened cell life.
2. Poor health with many bacterial, mental and psychosomatic illnesses. Acidic pH creates an increased susceptibility to germs.
3. A negative atmosphere is generated around you, which negatively affects those around you.
4. A shorter life span filled with unhappiness, misery and stress. Being occupied with problems eliminates creativity.
5. Destitution, poverty and indigence.
6. Unhappiness with an endless string of failures. When productivity is reduced the individual is completely in conflict with their own creative process and energies; role relationship becomes a contest between the individual's spirit, mind and body.

The negative syndrome is a continuum of fear, hatred and darkness, which are steps downward in emotional intensity. Every step is easy without effort and is usually done initially without derogatory reason, being the most logical thing to do in the world. The rationale behind the negative syndrome is easy to prove and the majority of humanity finds themselves snared within this dark side of subjective reality.[35] Most of this imprinting begins once again from 1st, 2nd and 3rd circuit disruptions in childhood, along with the social and genetic templates of each parent's primary cultural back ground for 7 generations. The negative

---

[35] (Powers)

syndrome is a continuum of mental illness and insanity

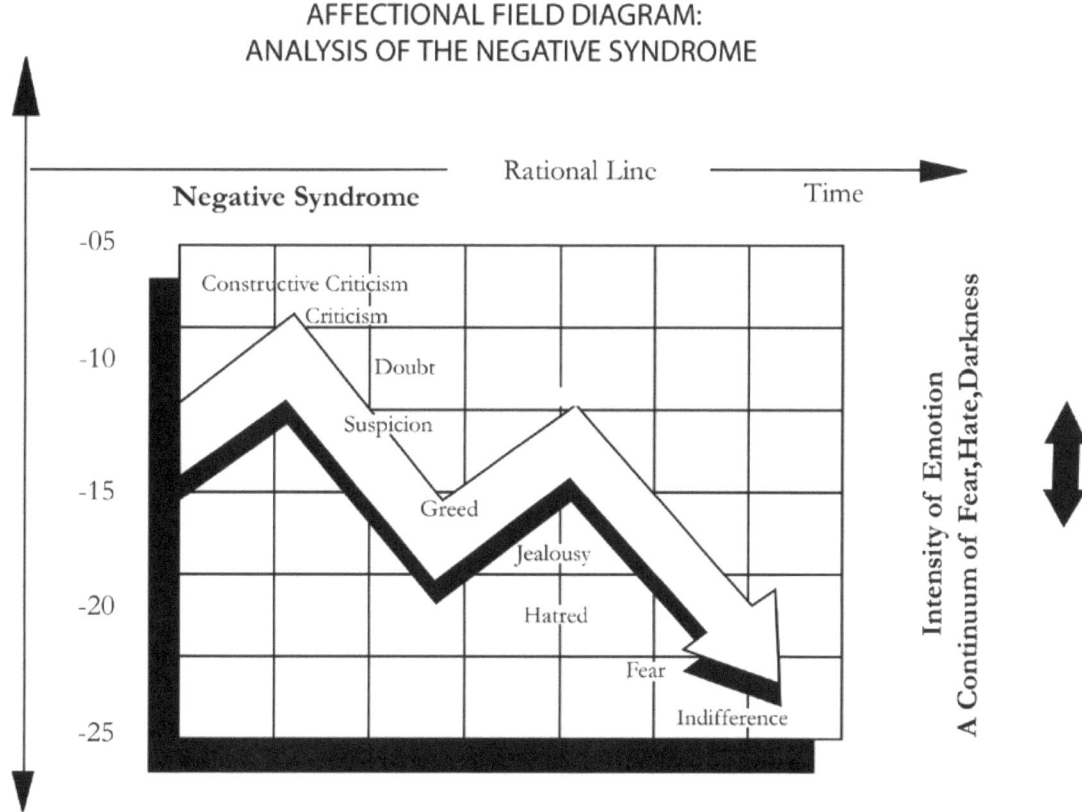

Results of feeling ANY of the Negative Emotions:

1. Generates a negative body Chemistry
   (Steam Bath, Litmus paper)
2. Shortens Cell Life …Shortens Your Life
3. More susceptible to Disease Germs
   (Flu, Colds etc.)
4. Creates a negative Atmospheres
   (Plant Experiments, Animals)
5. Eliminates Creativity
   (RAS occupied with problems)
6. Productivity sharply reduced
   (Happiness eliminated)

A healthy Philosophy:

Every time I go below the Rational Line I'm committing suicide – I'll NOT go below the line again! Every kind of weather is beautiful, all foods, are wonderful, all people are good – and I don't care how much proof you give me to the contrary – I won't accept it!!!

The positive aura is continuum of love, faith and light, which ranges from acknowledgment to affection of an unlimited nature, the 7 A's. It is a continuum of mental health that creates the following experiences of life:

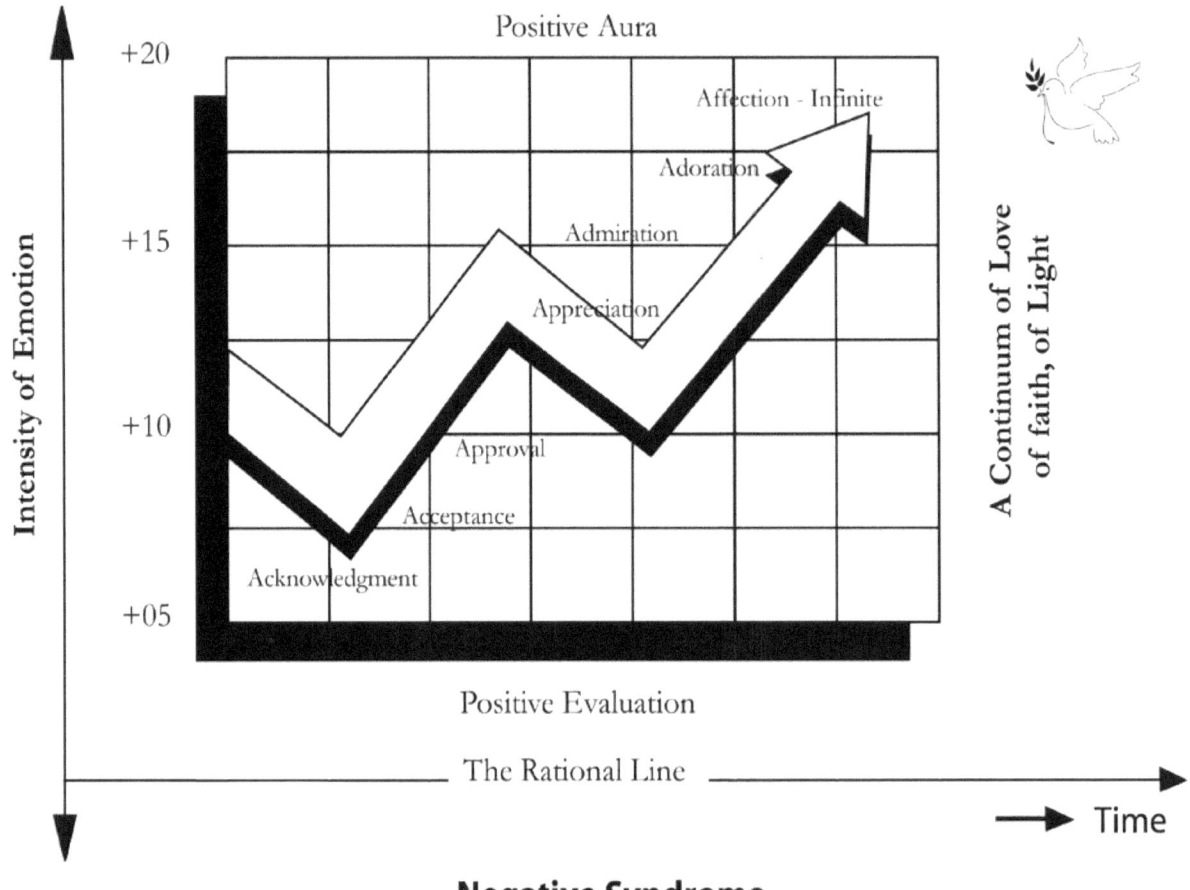

Negative Syndrome

Comparisons of the Characteristics of the Positive Aura and Negative Syndrome:
The Negative Syndrome is easy to prove . . . While the Positive Aura is difficult to prove. Every step downward step in the negative syndrome is easy, almost without effort; taken initially not for a derogatory reason; is the most logical thing in the world to do . . . Every step upward in the positive aura requires effort; every step upword defies logic; every step is illogical.

The negative syndrome is a continuum of metal illness & insanity . . . The Positive Aura is a continuum of mental health there is NO reality in the negative syndrome; it does not exist, its really only if you believe it's real . . . The only reason a being takes it's first breath is because of the reality of the positive Aura.

1. A positive body chemistry, resulting in extended cell life.
2. Excellent health with no bacterial, mental or psychosomatic illnesses. An alkaline pH promotes resistance to bacterial infections, common cold and viruses.
3. A positive atmosphere is generated around you positively affecting those around you. Consistent with the principle of Esho Funi.
4. A longer life filled with a degree of relative happiness and joy.
5. Happiness of fulfillment on the material plane and social prosperity; productivity via internal role relationship.

The only true realities exist within the bases of the positive aura, which is a continuum of faith, yet it is difficult to prove.[36] It is the nature of the human mind to move in the direction of disorder (Rational Realist down into the Negative Syndrome) when it is not focused on a specific object of positive influence or being guided under the constructive discipline and guidance of a true master (Male Role) of life who understands the profound nature of the 3 existences of past, present and future.

---

[36] (Powers)

AFFECTIONAL FIELD DIAGRAM: ANALYSIS OF POSITIVE AURA AND THE NEGATIVE SYNDROME

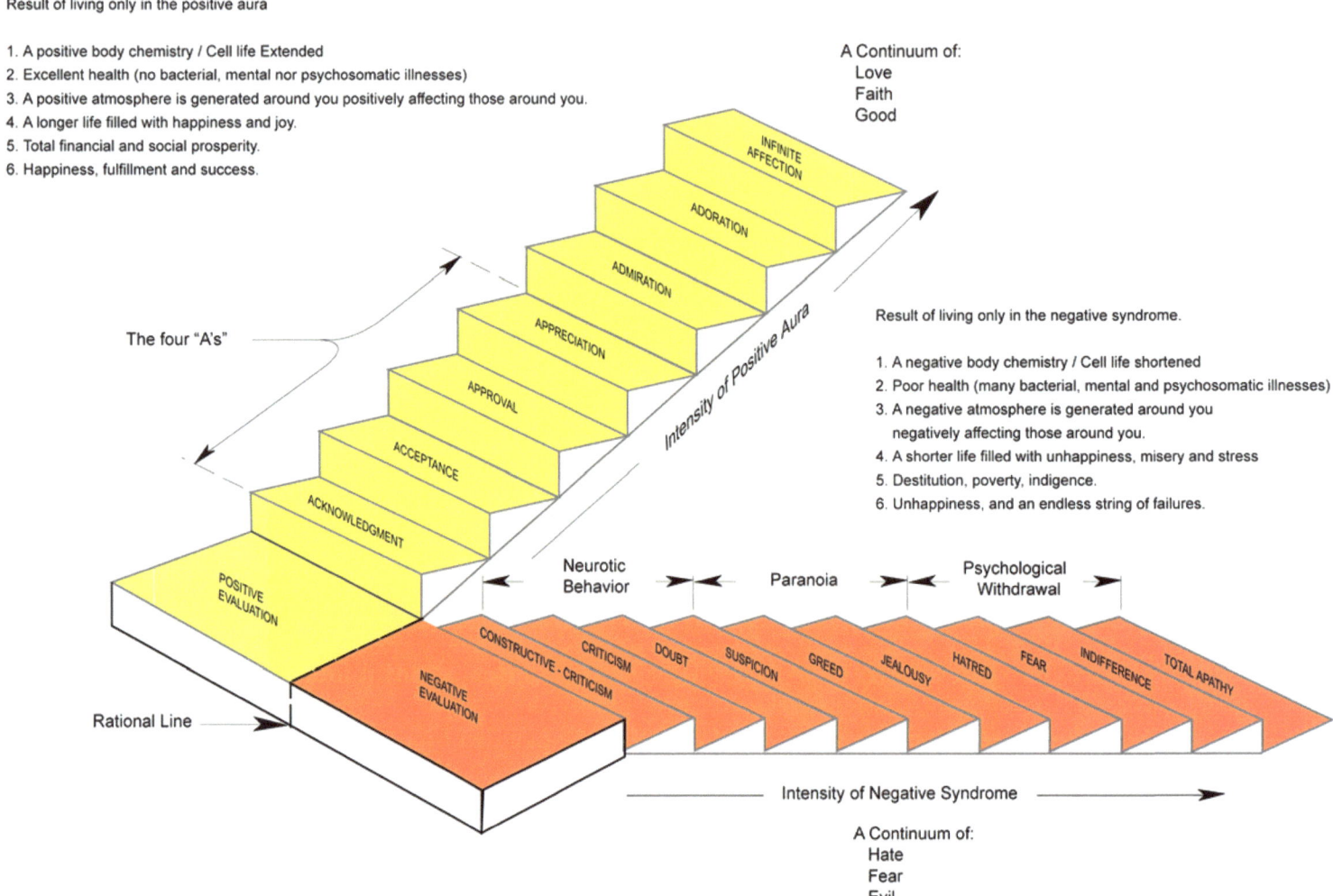

The Affective field is the complete spectrum of the degrees of human emotion that have shaped the planet's history and future events. Mastery of our subjective side of being therefore begins with the birth of faith, which is the non- logical aspiration of life in the positive aura. The effort to live and maintain ones' life on this side of the affectional field requires practice and complete awareness of the self. There are many different systems of analysis

that objectively illustrate the human experience on many levels. The two that are of particular interest here are the 5 personality patterns and the Buddhist principle of the Ten Worlds.

The five personality patterns consist of in ranking order the passive person, aggressive aggravator, rational realist, administrative assistant and the ideal individual. These personality patterns comprise psychological age groups that an individual functions from. (Fig. 8) The ideal individual is the completely mature adult that operate based on life's principles and is completely directed in consciousness by the realm of faith, the 7 A's. This individual is qualified to direct others as a leader within the ranks of humanity, based on his true level of spiritual evolution.

The 10 Worlds are the more profound of the two above descriptions of the human subjective experience. The 10 Worlds encompass both one's life and the environment as defined in chapter two's discussion on Ichinen Sanzen. Each world has its own distinctive experience, which can transform into any other of the 9 worlds, if given the right cause and condition.

Illustration

Basic Chart of Personality Patterns

Social Interaction	Passive Person	Aggressive Agrivator	Rational Realist	Administrative Assistant	Ideal Individual
Attitudes: Brain circuit Characterology Traits	Complaining, Whining, Negligence 1st Schizoid, Oral	Coercion (Bosses Others) Withhold, Argues, Raises Voice 1st, 2nd Psychopathic	Logic, Facts, Informational Authority, Debating 3rd Rigid	"Feels" for Others, Kinsetic, Mode Usual 4th Open Masochistic	Negotiation (Law of Fair Exchange), Love of Responsibility 4th, 5th, 6th, Open 7th
Systems:	Indifference (Value less than material)	Tyrannical (Inanimate Level)	Animate Level (Alone even in a team)	Paternal System (Humanitarian)	Role Relationships
Cognizance:	Closed Minded Level (No Submission)	Closed Minded Level (No Submission)	Open Minded Level (Acceptance) Both sides	Confidence Level (Partial Submission if Reward with A's)	Belief Level (Perfect Submission in the Female Role)
Values:	Passiveness (No Values)	Contest (Intimidation values)	Contest (Equalitarian Values)	1st 4 A's on the Affectional Field	7 A's on The Affectional Field
Method of Control:	None	Negative Persuasion, Manipulation Demand Authority	Informational Authority F. Role, Regulative A. Male Role	Emotional Coercion, F. Role, Positional Authority. Male role	Positive Persuasion & Acknowledged Authority from Others
Characteristic Emotion:	None	Hard	None (Fears Emotions)	Soft	Soft; Love for People Aggressive towards things & Elements
Primary Subconscious Fears	People, Ideas, Things, Event, Responsibility	Loss of Control, Illness, Involvement	Ambiguity, Affection, Involvement	Loss of 1st 4 A's..Judgement, Criticism	Operates on Principles, Does right in spite of FEAR

Continuing

Fig. 8

Personality Patterns

Illustration

	Basic Chart of Personality Patterns				
Social Interaction	Passive Person	Aggressive Agrivator	Rational Realist	Administrative Assistant	Ideal Individual
Reaction Under Stress	Psychological Withdrawal, Psychosis, Psychosomatic Illnesses Schizoid	Anxiety, Frustration, Tension, Neurosis, Paranoia	Physically Retreat, Withdrawal, Regression	"Mother Hen" Retreat, Regression Masochist	Leadership, Takes Command, Knowledge, Empathy, Wisdom, Courage
Their Belief Systems:	None	Air, Food, Water, Shelter, Sex, Security	Rules, Systems, Achievements, Pseudo, Perfection Rigid	The "BIG THEY" What others think of THEM	Structure within Self Right Relatedness to a "GOOD" Person
Goals:	None	Power, Control: (Psychopathy) Material Ownership, To be Physically Tough	Exactness, Perfection, Expertness Rigid	Loyalty to a Leader or Group 2nd, 3rd Circuit	Balanced Maturity, Help Others, Self-Actualization
Program Allowing Change:	Total Personality Revamp, Learning to Love, Relaxation	Learning to Value People more Than Things	Acceptance of more than one Variable, Recognizing Fallacy of Perfectionism	Elimination of the FEAR of What Others Think of THEM	Constant Weeding of Negativism, Love of Neg. Feedback, Arrive at Need Though Knowledge
Functional Positions:	Welfare, Social Programs, Chronic Unemployment	"Bosses" Construction, Carpenters, Mechanics Truck Drivers Etc.	Engineers, Draftsmen Lawyers, Accountants, Scientists	Clergy (Humanitarian) Elementary School teachers, Housewives, Nurses, Social Workers	Clergy, Psychologists, Professors, Executives, Leaders
Ideal Psychological Age:	Birth - 2 Years Old	2 – 6 Years Old	7 – 12 years Old	12 – 30 Years Old	30 + Years Old

Fig. 8-1

Hell is the lowest of the 10 Worlds and is described as one of the three evil paths. It is the realm of utmost suffering characterized by extreme mental or physical suffering with an impulse of rage to destroy oneself and everything else in the process. Hunger is the second world and is situated within the three evil paths. It is a state in which one is ruled by an insatiable desire for food, wealth, fame, power, or some other object or condition. When in this state one is tormented physically and spiritually by relentless craving. The cause for this state is attributed to tendencies such as greed, miserliness and jealousy. Animality the third of the three evil paths is a state in which one is swayed by instinctive desires and has no sense of reason or morality. The Daishonin describe this state as follows: "The short are swallowed by the long, and the small are eaten by the large, feeding upon each other without pause."[37]

Anger the fourth of the Ten Worlds is sometimes referred to as an evil path. It is dominated by a selfish ego that values oneself alone and holds others in contempt. A person in this life condition is attached to the idea of his own superiority and cannot bear to be inferior to others in anything.

Humanity is a state in which man has control over his instinctive desires with reason and acts in a humane fashion. In this state individuals have the rationale to distinguish good from evil and right from wrong of various matters, as opposed to the preceding 4 Worlds of Hell, Hunger, Animality and Anger (Asura) which only have desire without rational. The World of Humanity is said to be the state of calmness or composure. Yet this state of calmness is still shrouded in the illusions of darkness, for common mortals do not see the

---

[37] (The Gosho Translation Committee, 92)

dangers that exist just before them in life that are hidden from sight, because their spiritual eyes are closed. It is the ignorance of what is to come that allows them to be calm while making grave negative causes that invite suffering for their future. People know the words of cause and effect yet they calmly make evil causes while they enjoy themselves not knowing what those causes will bring them in the future. Our understanding of cause and effect is limited to what we research and believe about the functions within the environment, not human life itself. We have lost our true relationship with nature and ourselves because of false religious principles that distort these fundamental truths around and within us.

Heaven which is also known as rapture is the sixth of the Ten Worlds. It is the condition of joy that one experiences upon achieving the satisfaction of desires or upon release from pain. The joys of this state, of whatever kind, are transient and vulnerable to external circumstances.

The above conditions are called the Lower Six Worlds or the 6 paths of the Ten Worlds, which are controlled by earthly desires and are governed by an ever changing environment. The Four Noble Worlds comprise the worlds of learning, realization, bodhisattva and Buddhahood (Enlightenment). These worlds all require constant effort from the individual to maintain, the first 3 of which still remain in the realm of delusion under the influence of the fundamental darkness. Only the force or power of Buddhism can free an individual from the influence of the fundamental darkness. The powers of Buddhism to save all living beings are divided into 4 distinctive aspects.

1. The power of the Buddha- his compassionate actions to save all people with his spiritual strength and wisdom in the form of teachings of truth.

2. The power of the Law- the boundless force of the Mystic Law to lead all people to enlightenment.

(These two powers above are contained within the Dai Gohonzon)

3. The power of faith- the strength of one's resolve to remain focused upon the true object of influence (Gohonzon) throughout one's life, overcoming the influence of the fundamental darkness (it is a function of time and intention). The Daishonin states concerning the above, "Only when one encounters great persecutions can we know that he has truly mastered the Lotus Sutra." MWND vol. 3 pg.222 He also states in <u>The Receipt of New Fiefs</u>, "Faith in the Lotus Sutra acts as a prayer to attain Buddhahood. Above all, strengthen your seeking mind for the Way even further, so that you can attain Buddhahood in this lifetime." MWND Vol. 6 pg.263

4. The power of practice- the dynamic action of carrying out the physical activities of Buddhism, which encompasses Gongyo and Shodai for oneself and shakubuku, which is the instructing of others in the correct teachings of the Buddha allowing them to overcome their roots of suffering, incorrect religious views (illusions).

The world of learning, the 7th of the Ten Worlds was originally termed voice hearers, which were individuals who directly listened to the Buddha's words of truth. It later was defined as those who developed an understanding of the impermanence of all things and attempts to free himself from the sufferings of the six paths (first 6 of the Ten Worlds) by seeking some lasting truth through the teachings of others. The highest stage of enlightenment within this world is called the level of Arhat; one who has defeated robbers and bandits. This means that he has successfully overcome the illusions of thought and desire and has nothing more to learn.

The 8th world is that of realization, in this world an individual comes to understand the truth of the impermanence of life's reality by observing the phenomenal world directly, as opposed to the world of learning requiring a direct teacher. Through this awareness one strives to free himself from the sufferings of the six paths by seeking some lasting truth through his own observations and efforts. The highest level of enlightenment achieved in this state is that of pratykabuddha. This state of existence along with that of Arhat have become the source of much confusion within the context of what the true meaning of the word enlightenment represents. Since Buddhahood and enlightenment have the same meaning, many people assume that there are many different paths to become "enlightened." To clarify this it must be understood that true complete enlightenment is the path of following the instructions of a person who is called a Buddha, not the teachings of individuals who are in the state of Arhat or pratykabudda. Individuals in these states may be able to manifest some or all of the 6 supernatural powers, however this in no way frees the living beings of this world from the influence of the fundamental darkness, which is inherent throughout the first 9 of the Ten Worlds including the states of Arhat and Pratykabuddha.

Bodhisattva is the 9th of the Ten Worlds, which is a state characterized by the compassion to dedicate oneself to task of saving others from their suffering. This person has the aspiration for Buddhahood and engages in altruistic practice (shakubuku), which is the mercy of the Buddha and his disciples to correct other's mistaken views of life and religion, ultimately leading them to the fundamental truth of Myoho.

Glossary

*Akunin jobutsu- enlightenment of evil people.

*Alaya consciousness- Also called storehouse consciousness or karma repository. It is the eighth of the nine consciousnesses. Located below the realm of conscious awareness, it is called the storehouse consciousness because all karma created in the present and previous lifetimes is stored here. The alaya-consciousness is regarded as that which undergoes the cycle of birth and death and forms the framework of individual existence. All the actions and experiences of life that take place through the first seven consciousnesses are accumulated as karma in this alaya-consciousness, which at the same time exerts an influence on the workings of the seven consciousnesses. (Nichiren Shoshu Internation Center, 1983)

*Alpha waves- (8-13 cycles per second) brain waves traced on ECG

*Amala consciousness- Also, free-of-defilement consciousness or pure consciousness, the ninth and deepest of the nine consciousnesses. Amala means pure or undefiled, and vijnana means discernment. The eight consciousnesses set forth in the Consciousness-Only doctrine consist of the six consciousnesses (discernment by eyes, ears, nose, tongue, body, and mind), the mano-con-sciousness, and the alaya-consciousness. To these the Summary of the Mahayana (Chin She-lun; Jpn Shoron) school founded by Paramartha (499-569), the Flower Garland (Hua-yen; Kegon) school founded by Tu-shun (557-640), and the T'ien-t'ai (Jpn Tendai) school added a ninth consciousness, which is defined as the basis of all of life's functions. While the eighth or alaya-consciousness contains karmic impurities, the amalaconsciousness is pure, free from all defilement, and corresponds to the Buddha nature. (Nichiren Shoshu International Center, 1983)

*Amenea- healing system that works on bringing out the emotional energies held in the body.

    1. Heart area- giving and receiving for self

    2. Back problems- area were fear is held.

    3. Lungs- connected to tiredness of life and birth issues, holds blocks that prevent oxygen from going to the brain.

        *tacking in life force

        *child holds breath- emotions held in lungs

    4. Neck- childhood tapes held by child here

Emotionally charged sites draw accidents to the site of the energy.

***Ascension-** Means to move from a physically based reality to a consciousness based reality. (Brennan, 1999-2000 Workbook Junior, 1996)

***Asura-** A type of demon in Indian mythology. Contentious and belligerent, asuras fight continually with the gods. Buddhist scriptures often regard asuras as enemies of the gods, especially of Shakra, or Indra. Asuras are one of the eight kinds of nonhuman beings. The world of asuras is counted as one of the six paths, or the six lower states of existence among the Ten Worlds (anger). (Nichiren Shoshu Internation Center, 1983)

***Auric field-** defined by Barbara Brennan as the following; "From a scientific perspective, nobody has really proven what it is, so I can only talk from the perspective of a healer who works with it. I have a scientific background, but in fact there aren't any adequate experiments to tell you what the field really is. So, I am going to have to speak solely from my experience as a healer who is able to perceive the field. From this perspective, the human energy field is the matrix structure upon which the cells of the physical body grow. It is the template of the physical body.

It is also the vehicle for psychosomatic reactions, or the "mind-body" connection. The human energy field can be perceived by anyone with practice. It's of vital importance since it is a foundation for the physical body. It is directly connected with health and illness. Based upon my experience as a healer conducting private sessions with clients spanning a fifteen year period, and as a teacher for as many, I can tell you that anything that happens in the physical body will happen in the pattern of the energy fields first.

So the energy field precedes the physical body. It sets the foundation for the physical body, and anything that goes wrong in the energy field will eventually make its way into the physical body." (Brennan, Hands of Light, 1988)

***Awakening-** the process of moving from a physically based reality to a consciousness based reality, moving our self-orientation from the space-time coordinates into our individual core essence, this occurs through the three processes of transformation, transcendence and transfiguration. (Brennan, 1999-2000 Workbook Junior, 1996)

***Brennan, Barbara-** Barbara Brennan is a world-renowned spiritual leader, healer and educator. A pioneer and innovator in the field of energy consciousness, the former NASA physicist has been researching and exploring the Human Energy Field and realms of human consciousness for more than 30 years. She holds a Doctorate of Philosophy, a Doctorate of Theology, a Master's Degree in Atmospheric Physics, B.S. in Physics, and worked as a research scientist at NASA's Goddard Space Flight Center. She is also a graduate of the Institute of Core Energetics and Senior Pathwork® Helper.

Her best-selling books HANDS OF LIGHT® and LIGHT EMERGING are considered classics in the field of complementary medicine.

Dr. Brennan's first book, HANDS OF LIGHT: A Guide to Healing Through the Human Energy Field, was distinguished as Bantam's New Age best-seller in 1989. This landmark work on spiritual healing is published in 22 languages and has over a million copies in print. Her second book, LIGHT EMERGING: The Journey of Personal Healing, is also a best-seller and is published worldwide.

***Baines, John** - Dr. Salas began publishing his philosophy in 1966, under the literary pseudonym of John Baines, and quickly received acclaim for works such as *The Secret Science, The Stellar Man, Does Woman Exist?, Depression and Anguish, The Development of the Inner World, The Science of Love, Hypso-Consciousness* and *Morals for the 21st Century*. His central theme focuses upon the ongoing development of the individual to attain greater levels of awareness in order to achieve true success in all forms. As a practical objective, Dr. Salas' philosophy aims to guide the modern man and woman in finding their psychic way back to their birthright, of which life in the "fast lane" has robbed them, namely, an inner tranquility. His writing style is at once straightforward, clear and precise, accounting for his universal appeal. At present, Dr. Salas divides his year into days spent writing and lecturing in his hometown of Santiago and lecture tours abroad in other South American cities, The United States, Russia, and Spain. ✦**Facts about Dr. Dario Salas Sommer**

- In 1961, Dr. Salas founded the **Institute for Hermetic Philosophy (IHP)** in Santiago, Chile.
- Dr. Salas has given over **2,000 keynote speeches**, which have been heard worldwide, and he has been interviewed on international television and in magazines.
- Dr. Salas is the author of **8 books**, five of which have been translated into English, under the literary pseudonym of **John Baines**. His books have been translated into 8 different languages with over 1 million copies sold worldwide.
- Dr. Salas published *Morals for the 21st Century*, in which he elucidates his concept of **Moral Physics™**-- the innate relationship between moral values and natural laws. Dr. Salas established a laboratory with the express purpose of furthering his work with Moral Physics ™, using scientific experiments to demonstrate philosophical and moral precepts.
- On September 26, 2003, Dr. Salas was awarded an **honorary Doctorate in Philosophy**, and appointed Scientific Consul of Russia for all Latin America, **Knight of Arts and Sciences by the Academy of Natural Sciences of The Russian Federation**. He was also presented with the prestigious V.I.Vernadsky gold prize by Vladimir **Platanov**, the President of Moscow's Parliament (DUMA), for the role of his work in safeguarding the human being's psychological and physical integrity.

***Bishamon-** protects the place where the Buddha preaches and listens.

***Bliss body-** (one of 3) reward body or property of wisdom a Buddha possesses.

Buddha nature- internal cause or potential for attaining Buddhahood, which all people possess. Our Buddha nature communicates with the Buddha nature (seed) of the Gohonzon, beyond the perceptual range of the mental functions of the 6 lower consciousnesses.

Buddhist precept- "to stem injustice and stop evil" within oneself.

Bukkai soku kukai- Buddhahood possesses all nine worlds.

Central nervous system- the brain together with its extension the spinal cord, which receives and sends messages, interprets stores and coordinates those messages and makes decisions. Communication between the central nervous system and all organs of the body is via the peripheral nervous system, which consists of nerve pathways specialized for different purposes.

Defense system- is a protective reaction built into an individual's behavior which is automation, used when an individual feels threatened in some way and is a reaction to protect/ cover the wound. (Brennan, 1999-2000 Workbook Junior, 1996)

Demon-Also, evil demon, evil spirit, or simply spirit. Evil beings who torment people. Indian mythology and Buddhist scriptures mention various kinds of demons, such as rakshasa, yaksha, and kumbhanda. The "Encouraging Devotion" (thirteenth) chapter of the Lotus Sutra, for example, states: "In a muddied kalpa, in an evil age there will be many things to fear. Evil demons will take possession of others and through them curse, revile, and heap shame on us. But we, reverently trusting in the Buddha, will put on the armor of perseverance. In order to preach this sutra we will bear these difficult things." Demon also means negative functions or influences that deprive people of happiness or vitality, and obstruct correct judgment. In contrast with the function of gods that protect people's welfare, demons indicate forces in the environment that act to prevent or destroy human happiness. In Great Concentration and Insight, T'ien-t'ai (538-597) regarded attack by demons as one of the six causes of illness. (Nichiren Shoshu Internation Center, 1983)

Devil-A personification of evil. The Sanskrit word mara also means killing, death, pestilence, or obstacle, and in China it was translated as "robber of life." In Buddhist scriptures, Mara is the name of a devil king who rules over numerous devils who are his retinue. He is described as the great evil enemy of Shakyamuni Buddha and his teachings. When Shakyamuni entered into meditation under the bodhi tree, Mara attempted to prevent him from attaining enlightenment but failed. After Shakyamuni's enlightenment, he also tried to induce the Buddha to abandon his intent to preach. Mara is identified with the devil king of the sixth heaven. The sixth heaven is the highest heaven in the world of desire, or the Heaven of Freely Enjoying Things Conjured by Others, and its ruler delights in manipulating others to submit to his will. In Buddhism, devils indicate those functions that block or hinder people's effort to complete their Buddhist practice. (Nichiren Shoshu Internation Center, 1983)

*Deities- functions that bring disasters to those who do not protect Buddhism. Devils and deities are functions of the same phenomena (non duality)
  1. Evil people- punish
  2. Good people- protection

They also give Buddhist hard training and protection for the path to attain Buddhahood.

*Divine will- is a template or pattern for the great evolutionary plan of humanity and the universe. This template is alive, pulsating and constantly unfolding. It has a powerful, almost inexorable feeling of will and purpose. It is the experience of perfect order. When the individual is aligned with this level of universal order, they feel and experience the power and connectedness of being in sync with their greater purpose in time and space. (Brennan, 1999-2000 Workbook Junior, 1996)

*DNA- deoxyribonucleic acid, is the hereditary material in humans and almost all other organisms. Nearly every cell in a person's body has the same DNA. Most DNA is located in the cell nucleus (where it is called nuclear DNA), but a small amount of DNA can also be found in the mitochondria (where it is called mitochondrial DNA or mtDNA).

The information in DNA is stored as a code made up of four chemical bases: adenine (A), guanine (G), cytosine (C), and thymine (T). Human DNA consists of about 3 billion bases, and more than 99 percent of those bases are the same in all people. The order, or sequence, of these bases determines the information available for building and maintaining an organism, similar to the way in which letters of the alphabet appear in a certain order to form words and sentences.

DNA bases pair up with each other, A with T and C with G, to form units called base pairs. Each base is also attached to a sugar molecule and a phosphate molecule. Together, a base, sugar, and phosphate are called a nucleotide. Nucleotides are arranged in two long strands that form a spiral called a double helix. The structure of the double helix is somewhat like a ladder, with the base pairs forming the ladder's rungs and the sugar and phosphate molecules forming the vertical sidepieces of the ladder.

An important property of DNA is that it can replicate, or make copies of itself. Each strand of DNA in the double helix can serve as a pattern for duplicating the sequence of bases. This is critical when cells divide because each new cell needs to have an exact copy of the DNA present in the old cell. (Medicine)

*Dosho and Domyo – 2 gods on a person's shoulders that record all good and evil acts, then report them to King Emma, specifically this represents the law of cause and effect.
  Dosho- female on the right shoulder reports evil
  Domyo- male on the left reports good deeds

*E of Eho- means to depend; meaning living beings are dependent on their environment.

*Eho- objective world or insentient environment.

*Eight Winds-Eight conditions that prevent people from advancing along the right path to enlightenment. According to The Treatise on the Stage of Buddhahood Sutra-Bandhuprabha's work that was translated into Chinese by Hsüan-tsang-the eight winds are prosperity, decline, disgrace, honor, praise, censure, suffering, and pleasure. People are often swayed either by their attachment to prosperity, honor, praise, and pleasure (collectively known as "four favorites" or "four favorable winds"), or by their aversion to decline, disgrace, censure, and suffering ("four dislikes" or "four adverse winds"). (Nichiren Shoshu Internation Center, 1983)

*Eight phases of a Buddha's existence:

1. Descending from heaven

2. Entering his mother's body

3. Emerging from his mother's body

4. Renouncing the world

5. Conquering devils

6. Attaining enlightenment

7. Turning the wheel of the law

8. Entering nirvana

*Esho funi-Also, non-duality of life and its environment. The principle that life and it's environment though two seemingly distinct phenomena, are essentially non-dual; they are two integral phases of a single reality. In the Japanese term esho-funi, esho is a compound of shoho, meaning life or a living being, and eho, its environment. Funi, meaning "not two," indicates oneness or non-duality. It is short for nini-funi, which means "two (in phenomena) but not two (in essence)." Ho of shoho and eho means reward or effect. It indicates that "life" constitutes a subjective self that experiences the effects of its past actions, and "its environment" is an objective realm in which individuals' karmic rewards find expression. Each living being has its own unique environment. The effects of karma appear in oneself and in one's objective environment, because self and environment are two integral aspects of an individual. The Treatise on the Great Perfection of Wisdom by Nagarjuna (c. 150-250) introduces the concept of the three realms of existence, which views life from three different standpoints and explains the manifestation of individual lives in the real world. These three are the realm of the five components of life, the realm of living beings, each as a temporary combination of these components, and the realm of the environment. T'ien-t'ai (538-597) included this concept in his doctrine of three thousand realms in a single moment of life. According to Miao-lo's Annotations on "The Profound Meaning of the Lotus Sutra," two of these three realms-the realm of the five components and the realm of living beings-represent "life," and, naturally, the realm of the environment represents "environment" in terms of the principle of oneness of life and its environment. These three realms exist in a single moment of life and are inseparable from one another. Therefore, a living being and its environment are non-dual in their ultimate reality. Nichiren (1222-1282) writes in his letter On Omens: "The ten directions are the 'environment' and living beings are 'life.' To illustrate, environment is like the shadow, and life, the body. Without the body, no shadow can exist, and without life, no environment. In the same way, life is shaped by its environment". He also writes in On Attaining Buddhahood in This Lifetime: "If the minds of living beings are impure, their land is also impure, but if their minds are pure, so is their land. There are not two lands, pure or impure in themselves. The difference lies solely in the good or evil of our minds" (4). (Nichiren Shoshu Internation Center, 1983)

1. Fukaihon' I no jobutsu- attaining Buddhahood without change of original status (insentient beings)

1. Done through the influence of esho funi from a sentient beings Buddhahood.
2. By being made into an object of worship paper or wood.

2. Mokue niyo no jobutsu- the enlightenment of wooden or painted images Gohonzon

*Five delusion passions- Greed, anger, stupidity, arrogance and doubt.

*Five elements- earth (solid), water (liquid), fire (heat), wind (gas) and space (ku); space – an integration of the other four elements.

*Five guides for propagation: 1. The teaching 2.The People's capacity. 3. The time. 4. The country. 5. The sequence of propagation.

*Five types of vision:

1. Common mortal's eyes which distinguishes color and form.

2. The divine eye or the ability of heavenly beings to see beyond the physical limitations of darkness, distance or obstruction

3. The eyes of wisdom- the ability of those in the two vehicles to perceive that all phenomena are without substance

4. Eye of the Law- bodhisattvas use to penetrate all teachings in order to save the people.

5. Eye of the Buddha- which perceives the true nature of life spanning past, present and future. The eye of the Buddha includes all other four visions.

First Law of Thermodynamics- "The conservation of energy" states that energy can be neither created nor destroyed. Mass and energy may be converted one to the other.

Five components of life- Form, perception, conception volition and consciousness.
- Shiki- (form) physical aspect of life, which contains the five sense organs of eyes, ears, nose, tongue and body(tactile feeling) used for perception
- Ju- (perception) is the function of receiving external information through the six sense organs. The above five senses and the mind comprises the six sense organs.
- So- (conception) is the creation of mental ideas or conceptions about what has been perceived.
- Gyo- (volition) is the will which acts on the conception and motivates action towards what has been perceived.
- Shiki- (consciousness) is the function of discernment, and gives rise to the components of perception, conception and volition.

Form (shiki) represents the physical aspect of life and the other four components represent the spiritual aspect (shinpo).

Five elements- According to ancient Indian belief, the five constituents of all things in the universe. They are earth, water, fire, wind, and space. The first four correspond respectively to the physical states of solid, liquid, heat, and gas. Space is interpreted as integrating and harmonizing the other four elements.

Five false views- 1. Though the body is no more than a temporary union of the five components, one mistakenly regards the self as absolute and though nothing in the universe can belong to an individual one mistakenly views everything around him as his own possession. 2. One erroneously believes either that his life and the lives of others will end at death, or that they will continue after death in some eternally unchanging form such as the soul. 3. One does not recognize the law of cause and effect. 4. One adheres to one's misconceptions so bigotedly that one regards inferior things as superior. 5. One views erroneous practices or percepts as the true way to enlightenment.

Four forms of birth:

1. Birth from the womb, with mammals

2. Birth from eggs

3. Birth from moisture

4. Birth by transformation- beings and deities in hell

*Four debts of gratitude- debts owed to one's parents to all living beings, to one's sovereign and to the three treasures of Buddhism (The Buddha, the Law and the Priest).

*Four fearlessnesses- four aspects of the Buddha's fearlessness in preaching.

1. In declaring that he is enlightened to the truth of all phenomena

2. In proclaiming that he has extinguished all desires and illusions.

3. In teaching that desires and karma can be obstacle to enlightenment.

4. In teaching that one can overcome all suffering by practicing Buddhism.

*Four noble truths- 1. All existence is suffering; 2. Suffering is caused by selfish craving; 3. The eradication of selfish cravings brings about the cessation of suffering and enables one to attain nirvana; and 4. There is a path by which this eradication can be achieved, namely, the discipline of the eight-fold path. (Nichiren Shoshu Internation Center, 1983)

*Four Powers of Buddhism- The power of the Buddha, the power of the Law, the power of faith, and the power of practice. In Nichiren's teachings, the four powers are known as the four powers of the Mystic Law, whose interaction enables one to have one's prayers answered and attain Buddhahood. The power of the Buddha is the Buddha's compassion in saving all people. The power of the Law indicates the boundless capacity of the Mystic Law to lead all people to enlightenment. The power of faith is to believe in the Gohonzon, the object of devotion that embodies the power of the Buddha and the power of the Law, and the power of practice is to chant Nam-myoho-renge-kyo oneself and teach others to do the same. To the extent that one brings forth one's powers of faith and practice, one can manifest the powers of the Buddha and the Law within one's own life. The power of self, the power of another, the power of good karma, and the power of expedient means. The four powers expounded in the Upholding the Bodhisattva Stage Sutra that enable one to arouse the aspiration for enlightenment. The power of self means arousing the aspiration for enlightenment through one's own devoted effort in practice. The power of another means, arousing the aspiration for enlightenment through being taught and inspired by another. The power of good karma means that, because of one's practice of the great vehicle teaching in past existences and because of good causes accumulated thereby, one encounters a Buddha or bodhisattva in this lifetime and so conceives the aspiration for enlightenment. The power of expedient means indicates that one seeks a good friend or teacher who skillfully expounds the Buddha's teaching in the way best suited to one's capacity, thus awakening in one the desire for enlightenment. (Nichiren Shoshu Internation Center, 1983)

*Four A's- first 4 levels of the intensity of the positive Aura within the affectional field. (Powers)

*Four Standards- Also, four reliances. The Four standards that Buddhists must follow, according to the Nirvana Sutra and the Vimalakirti Sutra, the four standards are (1) to rely on the Law and not upon persons; (2) to rely on the meaning of the teaching and not upon the words; (3) to rely on wisdom and not upon discriminative thinking; and (4) to rely on sutras that are complete and final and not upon those that are not complete and final. (Nichiren Shoshu Internation Center, 1983)

*Fourteen slanders: 1. Arrogance 2. negligence 3. arbitrary, egotistical judgment 4. shallow self-satisfied understanding 5. attachment to earthly desires 6. lack of seeking spirit 7. not believing 8. aversion 9. deluded doubt 10. vilification 11.contempt 12. hatred 13. jealousy and 14. grudges.

*Four types of auric field dynamics- are the four ways an individual can regulate the activities of the HEF.

    1. Push

    2. Pull

    3. Hold

    4. Allow

*Four types of people present when the Buddha expounds his Law.

    1. Questioners (Hokkishu): Those who ask the Buddha questions, or beg him to teach the law, thus helping expound his law.

    2. Sympathizers (Tokishu): Those who understand and become convinced of the Buddha's teachings.

    3. Listeners (Kechienshu): Those who listen to the teachings of the Buddha and later attain enlightenment.

    4. Assistants (Yogoshu): Those who always follow the Buddha wherever he teaches the law and prove that his teachings are true. (Toda, 1968)

*Frequencies of Brilliance- is a process that opens you up to receiving birthing frequencies of Remembrance that activate all cells throughout the body, awakening new areas of the brain, completing DNA re-patterning, and emerging into a new truth and frequency of reality. This process changes the frequencies of the body and prepares us for the transition to higher dimensions of consciousness. This is done on the physical body or just above the body, through a series of doorways that hold the purest frequencies of Remembrance of Truth. This process allows us to bypass the illusion of our three dimensional reality, allowing us to directly experience the True Light that is here for us to live and be. Awakening occurs on a physical and spiritual level, within your body and within your world.

*Fundamental Darkness-Also, fundamental ignorance or primal ignorance. The most deeply rooted illusion inherent in life, said to give rise to all other illusions. Darkness in this sense means inability to see or recognize the truth, particularly, the true nature of one's life. The term fundamental darkness is contrasted with the fundamental nature of enlightenment, which is the Buddha nature inherent in life. According to the Shrimala Sutra, fundamental darkness is the most difficult illusion to surmount and can be eradicated only by the wisdom of the Buddha. T'ien-t'ai (538-597) interprets darkness as illusion that prevents one from realizing the truth of the Middle Way, and divides such illusion into forty-two types, the last of which is fundamental darkness. This illusion is only extirpated when one attains the stage of perfect enlightenment, the last of the fifty-two stages of bodhisattva practice. Nichiren (1222-1282) interprets fundamental darkness as ignorance of the ultimate Law, or ignorance of the fact that one's life is essentially a manifestation of that Law, which he identifies as Nam-myoho-renge-kyo. In The Treatment of Illness, Nichiren states: "The heart of the Lotus school is the doctrine of three thousand realms in a single moment of life, which reveals that both good and evil are inherent even in those at the highest stage of perfect enlightenment. The fundamental nature of enlightenment manifests itself as Brahma and Shakra, whereas the fundamental darkness manifests itself as the devil king of the sixth heaven". Nichiren thus regards fundamental darkness as latent even in the enlightened life of the Buddha, and the devil king of the sixth heaven as a manifestation or personification of life's fundamental darkness. The Record of the Orally Transmitted Teachings reads, "Belief is a sharp sword that cuts off fundamental darkness or ignorance." (Nichiren Shoshu Internation Center, 1983)

*Ganges River- The great river of the northern and northeastern Indian subcontinent, which originates in the Himalayas and flows southeast across the vast Ganges Valley emptying into the Bay of Bengal through the Ganges Delta. Its length is about 2,500 kilometers. In Sanskrit the river is called Ganga. Depicted as a beautiful river goddess in Indian mythology, Ganga originally flowed only through heaven, but was brought to earth by the gods Brahma and Shiva. In Buddhist scriptures, the Ganges is counted as one of the four great rivers in Jambudvipa. The Rigveda, the earliest Vedic scripture, took root here and gave rise to India's Vedic religion and culture. The fertile Ganges Valley also supported a flourishing agriculture and commerce. Many cities were built and prospered in the Ganges Valley, which constituted the cradle and the center of successive Indian civilizations. Around the time of Shakyamuni, a number of new kingdoms emerged, the most powerful of which were Kosala in the middle Ganges Valley and Magadha in the lower Ganges Valley. Shakyamuni spread his teachings widely in the region, and his followers increased rapidly in number. As a result, monasteries were built in many cities in the valley. The Mauryan dynasty, renowned for its ruler Ashoka of the third century B.C.E., established the city of Pataliputra (present-day Patna) as the center of its empire on the banks of the Ganges. The Gupta dynasty, which began in the fourth century C.E., also made Pataliputra its capital.

The Ganges has long been held sacred, and today is still revered as a holy river by Hindus who believe that they can eradicate their sins by immersing themselves in its waters. Crematoriums have been built along the banks of the Ganges, and the Hindus cast the ashes of the dead into the river, believing this will deliver the deceased straight to heaven. Along the basin of the Ganges are some of the most prominent Indian cities, such as Varanasi (the holy city of the Hindus), Patna, and Calcutta on the bank of an arm of the Ganges River called the Hooghly. (Nichiren Shoshu Internation Center, 1983)

*Gohonzon- The object of worship in Nichiren Shoshu. Go is an honorific prefix in Japanese. Honzon means object of worship. All Gohonzons in Nichiren Shoshu are transcriptions of the Dai-Gohonzon made by the successive High Priests of Nichiren Shoshu.

*Happiness- means we have no fear in any kind of circumstance, exercising the inherent wisdom and action appropriate to the specifics of the situations one faces in life. People become aware of the true meaning of life and death.

*Harmonic Induction- within the HEF the individual with the stronger auric field exerts an influence over others. An individual who is very advanced spiritually or pure will establish an influence of order on the environment. In the practice of True Buddhism the high vibration to the realm of the Law transmits the influence of the Daishonin's living essence to those who purely focus on the Dai Gohonzon without obstructing this influence in the form of slanderous activities of mind, body and action as stated in the 14 slanders. The individual's auric field is lifted to the higher frequencies of vibration, that also releases the individuals personal process or karma that then has to be dealt with.

*Ho- means manifest effect; the karmic reward of a living being takes shape in its environment.

*Ho Honzon- the object of worship in terms of the Law, Dai Gohonzon. The Buddha can become any aspect of the environment such as wooden or painted images, in example ink from plants and wood from trees.

*ID point- the individuation point, which resides above the head and looks like an inverted funnel within the hara dimension. It carries the function of reason and our reason for incarnation, and through it we connect to our higher spiritual reality. (Brennan, Light Emerging, 1993)

***Ishin daie-** principle of substituting faith for wisdom in the practice of True Buddhism.

***Illusion-**Also, delusions of thought and desire. Errors or afflictions of perception and emotion that cause people to suffer in the lower realms or states of existence described as the six paths and the threefold world. People of the two vehicles are said to rid themselves of these illusions and gain freedom from rebirth in the threefold world. In general, the illusions of thought are regarded as distorted perceptions of reality, and the illusions of desire as base inborn inclinations such as greed, anger, and arrogance: (1) In the Dharma Analysis Treasury (Chin Chü-she; Jpn Kusha) school, the illusions of thought are described as those arising from ignorance of the four noble truths, and the illusions of desire as those arising from attachment. (2) In the Consciousness-Only school, the illusions of thought are regarded as those caused by erroneous teachers and misleading doctrines, and the illusions of desire as those inherent in life. (3) In the T'ien-t'ai school, illusions of thought and desire are one of three categories of illusion, the other two being illusions innumerable as particles of dust and sand and illusions about the true nature of existence.

***Image-** is a wrong or limiting belief about life, and the resulting clog to the energy field, blocks emotions and defensive attitudes that direct the misconception. It is the principle expression of our dualistic thinking which divides and limits life.

***Immutable karma-** Karma which produces a fixed result, which has four causes; **1.** Actions motivated by exceptionally strong earthly desires or by a profoundly pure mind.

    2. Actions, whether good or evil, done habitually.

    3. Actions, whether good or evil, performed vis-à-vis such sources of benefit as the three treasures.

    4. Actions causing harm to one's parents.

Immutable karma is also interpreted as karma whose effects are destined to appear at a fixed time, which has three types;

    1. Karma whose effects are destined to appear in the same lifetime.

    2. Karma whose effects are destined to appear in the next lifetime.

    3. Karma whose effects are destined to appear in a third or even later lifetime.

Lighter karma manifest itself in the same life it was created. Exceptionally bad karma will be carried over into subsequent lifetimes. (Nichiren Shoshu Internation Center, 1983)

Issho jobutsu- to attain Buddhahood in this lifetime.

Jinriki chapter (21st) - Shakyamuni transferred the Law to the Bodhisattvas of the Earth in this chapter of the the Lotus sutra.

Koku fudoe- "the infinite and stable wisdom" is what Nichiren Daishonin's Buddhism's wisdom is called.

Loci of control- is a concept in psychology, originally developed by Julian Rotter in the 1950s. The two 'loci', as established by the theory, are the internal and external loci. The locus of control represents how a person's decision making ability is influenced; essentially, those who make choices primarily on their own are considered to have internal loci, while those who make decisions based more on what others desire are said to have external loci. People with external loci are generally more apt to be stressed and suffer from depression as they are more aware of work situations and life strains. Women tend to have more of an external locus than men. A more internal locus of control is generally seen as desirable. Having an Internal locus of control can also be referred to as "personal control", "self-determination", etc. Males tend to be more internal than females; as people get older they tend to become more internal; People higher up in organizational structures tend to be more internal. Internal locus protects against submission to authority- more resistant to others influence (but tend to be more premature and less sympathetic than externals). Locus of control is related to, but distinct from, several other social psychological constructs related to control. (Wikipedia, 2008)

Karma- Potentials in the inner, unconscious realm of life created through one's actions in the past or present that manifest themselves as various results in the present or future. Karma is a variation of the Sanskrit karman, which means act, action, a former act leading to a future result, or result. Buddhism interprets karma in two ways: as indicating three categories of action, i.e., mental, verbal, and physical, and as indicating a dormant force thereby produced. That is, one's thought, speech, and behavior, both good and bad, imprint themselves as a latent force or potential in one's life.

This latent force, or karma, when activated by an external stimulus, produces a corresponding good or bad effect, i.e., happiness or suffering. There are also neutral acts that produce neither good nor bad results. According to this concept of karma, one's actions in the past have shaped one's present reality, and one's actions in the present will in turn influence one's future. This law of karmic causality operates in perpetuity, carrying over from one lifetime to the next and remaining with one in the latent state between death and rebirth.

It is karma, therefore, that accounts for the circumstances of one's birth, one's individual nature, and in general the differences among all living beings and their environments. It was traditionally viewed as a natural process in which no god or deity could intervene. The Hindu gods, in fact, were subject to the same law of karma as people, having become gods supposedly through the creation of good karma. The idea of karma predates Buddhism and was already prevalent in Indian society well before the time of Shakyamuni. This pre-Buddhist view of karma, however, had an element of determinism, serving more to explain one's lot in life and compel one to accept it than inspiring hope for change or transformation. The Brahmans, who were at the top of the Indian class structure by birth, may well have emphasized this view to secure their own role. The idea of karma was further developed, however, in the Buddhist teachings.

Shakyamuni maintained that what makes a person noble or humble is not birth but one's actions. Therefore the Buddhist doctrine of karma is not fatalistic. Rather, karma is viewed not only as a means to explain the present, but also as the potential force through which to influence one's future. Mahayana Buddhism holds that the sum of actions and experiences of the present and previous lifetimes are accumulated and stored as karma in the depths of life and will form the framework of individual existence in the next lifetime. Buddhism therefore encourages people to create the best possible karma in the present in order to ensure the best possible outcome in the future. In terms of time, some types of karma produce effects in the present lifetime, others in the next lifetime, and still others in subsequent lifetimes. This depends on the nature, intensity, and repetitiveness of the acts that caused them. Only those types of karma that are extremely good or bad will last into future existences. The other, more minor, types will produce results in this lifetime. Those that are neither good nor bad will bring about no results.

Karma is broadly divided into two types: fixed and unfixed. Fixed karma is said to produce a fixed result-that is, for any given fixed karma there is a specific effect that will become manifest at a specific time. In the case of unfixed karma, any of various results or general outcomes might arise at an indeterminate time. Irrespective of these differences, the Buddhist philosophy of karma, particularly that of Mahayana Buddhism, is not fatalistic. No ill effect is so fixed or predetermined that good karma from Buddhist practice in the present cannot transform it for the better. Moreover, any type of karma needs interaction with the corresponding conditions to become manifest. (Nichiren Shoshu International Center, 1983)

*Kumarajiva-When Buddhism was introduced into China, it was necessary to translate the sutras into Chinese. The translators inaccurately used terms from Taoism and Confucianism, which unfortunately misled or confused the readers. Later, a number of monks with a thorough understanding of Chinese and other languages made new translations which preserved the original meanings of the sutras. The greatest of these monks was called Kumarajiva.

Kumarajiva (344D413) was from Kucha, a small ancient state in what is now Xinjiang Province in northwestern China. His father, Kumarayana, was an Indian prince. He preferred Buddhism to his wealthy royal life, so he left India and eventually reached Kucha. The king of Kucha had a sister who was about twenty years old. She was beautiful and intelligent and many men wanted to marry her, but she refused them all. However, when she saw Kumarayana, she immediately fell in love with him. The king gave him his sister in marriage, and one year later their son Kumarajiva was born.

While she was pregnant with Kumarajiva, the mother suddenly became more intelligent and her power of reasoning became stronger. She was also able to understand Sanskrit. Therefore, it was said that the child would indeed be extraordinary.

When Kumarajiva was seven years old, his mother left home to become a nun. The boy accompanied his mother to the temple. She thought he would want to go home after a few days, but to her surprise, he was fascinated by the Buddhist scriptures and did not want to go home at all. All these signs reminded her of the omens when she was pregnant. Thus, all the great minds were invited to the temple to teach the boy, and he showed his talent by reading and memorizing thousands of Buddhist verses.

Because mother and son were members of the royal family, they received special care and treatment. The mother worried that this would make her son lax in his Buddhist training, so she decided to take him elsewhere.

When the boy was nine years old, his mother took him from Kucha to Kubha, a state in what is now Kashmir, and had him study under Pantoutatuo, a famous Buddhist monk who was also the brother of the king of Kubha. After about two years, the king requested Kumarajiva's presence at the palace to debate with some religious sectarians who were challenging the Buddhists. At first these people did not think much of Kumarajiva because he was only eleven years old, but the boy was able to defeat them with his cool manner and intelligence.

The whole country went wild with the news. The exuberant king sent many gifts to Kumarajiva, even moving him to a larger room and having several monks and novices look after him. After some time, his mother again worried that such a life of luxury could hinder his spiritual cultivation and studies, so when he turned twelve years old, they left again for a kingdom called Shale.

When they arrived, they received a warm welcome because the people there had already heard of the boy's successful debate in Kubha. Kumarajiva spent his time reading all the Hinayana Buddhist scriptures. One day as he was wandering around Shale, he came across a prince named Sumo from the state of Shachu. This prince knew a great deal about the Mahayana Buddhist scriptures. When Kumarajiva talked with Sumo, he suddenly realized that the Hinayana philosophy was quite inferior and he decided to direct all his energy into learning Mahayana Buddhism.

As time passed, Kumarajiva became quite famous and his uncle, Paichun, who was now the king of Kucha, dispatched messengers to bring them back home. Paichun built a new temple where they lived and where Kumarajiva preached. In 363, Kumarajiva celebrated his twentieth birthday, at which he not only marked his adulthood, but also received all the precepts and became a real Buddhist monk. At this time, his mother decided that her son was now an adult and they had to go their own ways, so she went to India alone. She asked the young monk to go east to spread Buddhism, but she knew that his path would be filled with all sorts of difficulties.

From 304 to 439, China was ruled by a sequence of Chinese dynasties and was in a state of constant civil war. In 378, Fu Chien, the founding ruler of the Chien Chin state, had already heard of Kumarajiva and wanted him to assist in government affairs. He ordered his general, Lu Kuang, to go west and bring Kumarajiva back, but he warned him not to destroy Kucha. However, Lu Kuang did not obey and destroyed several states on his way to Kucha. In Kucha, he killed the king along with many other people, and installed the king's younger brother on the throne. When Lu Kuang saw that Kumarajiva was so young, he despised him deeply. Among other insults, the general forced the monk to drink alcohol and marry his cousin. The year was 384.

When they reached Liang Chou, they learned that Fu Chien had been killed by Yao Chang, one of his subjects. Lu Kuang then set up a state of his own and called it Hou Liang. After sixteen years, Yao Hsing, Yao Chang's son, attacked the state of Hou Liang and Kumarajiva was freed. The monk was then welcomed into the capital, Changan.

When Kumarajiva arrived in Changan, Yao Hsing, himself a Buddhist, invited many monks to join Kumarajiva in translating the scriptures. After Buddhism was introduced into China, many people had tried to translate the Buddhist texts into Chinese. Unfortunately, they used terms from Confucianism and Taoism to explain or substitute for Buddhist terms. The translated scriptures became distorted or unintelligible and it was thus necessary to retranslate them.

It was said that around eight hundred people helped Kumarajiva translate the scriptures. First, he would read a phrase in its original language to his assistants and translate it into Chinese. If everyone agreed with the translation, then the Chinese version was recorded. Anyone could raise questions about the translations. During his lifetime, Kumarajiva translated more than three hundred volumes of scriptures.

Kumarajiva seemed to have all his troubles behind him, but his happiness did not last. One day, Yao Hsing came and said that he had prepared a palace filled with women, because he wanted Kumarajiva to have children who could be as smart as their father and take over the work of propagating Buddhism and translating the scriptures. The monk then realized why his mother had told him that he would undergo many difficulties in spreading Buddhism. Although he accepted the palace and the women, he still retained his purity and faithfully kept the Buddhist precepts.

One day in 413, Kumarajiva suddenly fell ill. His disciples prayed for him for days, but it was useless. Knowing that his end was near, he told his disciples that he was delighted to have worked with them, and he also vowed that if any translation had been incorrect, his tongue would be burned during the cremation. Indeed, after his cremation, everyone was amazed to see that his tongue still remained among the ashes. Kumarajiva, one of the greatest translators of the Buddhist scriptures, died in Changan in 413, at the age of seventy. (Sen-shou, 2008)

***Kushan Empire**-The Kushans originated from the Turkistan region of China. They moved towards Afghanistan in the 1st century AD and after displacing the Indo-Greeks, the Parthians and the Sakas, they established themselves in Taxila and Peshawar. In the course of time, they occupied entire Punjab and took parts of the western Gangetic plains beyond Mathura. Mathura was an important city at the time of the Kushans. Soon the Kushan Empire spread from Central Asia in the north to the plains near Mathura.

Two successive Kushan dynasties ruled the Kushan Empire. Kanishka was an important king, who belonged to the second Kushan dynasty. He extended the Kushan Empire to the north to such an extent that he came into open conflict with the Chinese armies of the Hun Empire, in Central Asia. Kanishka was a great patron of Mahayana Buddhism and during his reign, a large number of Buddhist monasteries, sculptures, and stupas were built in the Gandhara region. He also took active part in religious debates, which went on at that time. The fourth Buddhist Council was held during his reign, where many important decisions pertaining to the future of Buddhism were taken.

In the fourth Buddhist Council, the division of Buddhist faith into two branches, namely Mahayana (the greater vehicle) and Hinayana (the lesser vehicle), was recognized and accepted. (Maps of India, 2008)

***Land of Eternal tranquil light-** Also, Land of Tranquil Light or Land of Eternal Light. The Buddha land, is free from impermanence and impurity. The Land of Eternally Tranquil Light is one of the four kinds of lands described in the doctrine of the T'ien-t'ai school, the other three being the Land of Sages and Common Mortals, the Land of Transition, and the Land of Actual Reward. In many sutras, this saha world is described as an impure land filled with delusions and sufferings, and the Buddha land as a pure land free from these and far removed from this saha world. In contrast, the Lotus Sutra reveals the saha world to be the Buddha land, or the Land of Eternally Tranquil Light, and explains that the nature of a land is determined by the minds of its inhabitants. (Nichiren Shoshu Internation Center, 1983)

***Law-** A **physical law**, **scientific law**, or a **law of nature** is a scientific generalization based on empirical observations of physical behavior. They are typically conclusions based on repeated scientific experiments over many years, and which have become accepted universally within the scientific community.

The production of a summary description of nature in the form of such laws is the fundamental aim of science. Laws of nature are distinct from the law, either religious or civil, and should not be confused with the concept of [natural law](). Moreover, "law of nature" and "proposition (or formula) expressing a law of nature" are often used synonymously. However, taken strictly, there is a difference between law-propositions (or formulas), which, qua being formulations of laws, are semiotic entities, and laws (of nature), which are non-semiotic entities. Laws of nature exist independently of their physical formulations. (Wikipedia, 2008)

***Law of Fair Exchange**- universal principle of the nature balance between efforts and reward and the exchange of labor for goods or a measure of monetary value between two or more individuals.

***Law of Conservation of Energy and Matter-** states that energy cannot be created or destroyed, but can change its form. The total quantity of matter and energy available in the universe is a fixed amount and never any more or less. (Wikipedia, 2008)

***Learning Systems-** are established in cultural settings were fluctuating attention is cast on lower order repetitive task involving rote memorization, which denigrates much of the learning that could potentially occur. These methods of learning are actually conditionings or programming, which are held in high esteem in human existence, and all revolve around knowledge, understanding, control and application of physical and energy based systems. This system of learning is all based on the input receive through the five senses, greatly eliminating the last vestiges of identity and self-cognition from the individual to evolve beyond 3rd circuit mentality. There are no directives guiding human mentation/consciousness away from the limitations of time-space physical matter other than the small number of "schools of ancient wisdom." The primary directive is towards human sociological history, which ignores the Source essence from which all life arises. (Valerian, 1992)

***Life pulse-** the four phases of the creative process that begins in the depths of the core star moving out into the hara, the aura and into the physical world as our expression of who we are in the form of behavioral action. It then returns from the physical back to its origin within the core star after we observe it in the highly polished mirror of the material world. (Brennan, 1999-2000 Workbook Junior, 1996)

***Mappo-**Also, age of the Decadent Law, age of the Final Law, or latter age. The last of the three periods- the Former Day of the Law, the Middle Day of the Law, and the Latter Day of the Law-following Shakyamuni Buddha's death, when his teachings are said to fall into confusion and lose the power to lead people to enlightenment. The Latter Day of the Law is said to last for ten thousand years. The fifth of five five-hundred-year periods following Shakyamuni's death described in the Great Collection Sutra corresponds to the beginning of the Latter Day of the Law. The sutra predicts that it will be an "age of quarrels and disputes," when monks will disregard the precepts and feud constantly among themselves, when erroneous views will prevail, and when Shakyamuni's teachings will "be obscured and lost."

In contrast, the Lotus Sutra views the Latter Day of the Law as the time when the teaching it contains will be propagated. The "Medicine King" (twenty-third) chapter of the Lotus Sutra says, "After I have passed into extinction, in the last five-hundred-year period you must spread it abroad widely throughout Jambudvipa and never allow it to be cut off." T'ien-t'ai (538-597) states in The Words and Phrases of the Lotus Sutra, "In the last five-hundred-year period, the mystic way will spread and benefit humankind far into the future," and Dengyo (767-822) says in An Essay on the Protection of the Nation, "The Former and Middle Days are almost over, and the Latter Day is near at hand." It was believed in Japan that the Latter Day would begin in 1052; this was based on an account in The Record of Wonders in the Book of Chou that places Shakyamuni's death in 949 B.C.E. Modern research suggests, however, that he died in the early fifth century B.C.E.

The concept of the Latter Day of the Law is also applied to Buddhas other than Shakyamuni, and Buddhist scriptures often refer to the "Latter Day of the Law" of a particular Buddha as the age in which that Buddha's teachings are lost. (Nichiren Shoshu Internation Center, 1983)

*Melanin- A skin pigment (substance that gives the skin its color). Dark-skinned people have more melanin than light- skinned people. Melanin also acts as a sunscreen and protects the skin from ultraviolet light.

Melanin is produced by cells called melanocytes. It provides some protection again skin damage from the sun, and the melanocytes increase their production of melanin in response to sun exposure, which occur in people of all races, are small, concentrated areas of increased melanin production.

*Morphic Field- is a unified field which is the soul of the cell surrounding the mass of the cell. It contains the soul memory within each of the cell unit. One cell contains info of the whole living structure (bio-system). A grid that interconnects all the fields of a given group via a unified field matrix that carries info signal at speeds faster than light, organizing all individual organism of a specific species to adjust and or adapt behavioral patterns. (Valerian, 1992)

*Morphic resonance- is the influence of like upon like through or across space or time. Its implication, in the realm of heredity, is that inheritance depends not only on the chemical genes coded in DNA but also on morphic resonance from past members of the species. Other implications are an accelerated rate of evolution of new patterns of form and behavior; memory in individuals being based on self-resonance and not stored in the brain; the existence of a collective memory, to which we all contribute and on which we all draw; and providing understanding of past-life memories, survival of bodily death, telepathy, and ritual.

This hypothesis is part of a wider change in paradigm in which all of Nature, the entire cosmos, is viewed as being alive. This new sense of the life of Nature connects with the morphic resonance idea in the idea of the memory of place, or field, exemplified by the sense of places both haunted and sacred, which is the basis of such human activities as pilgrimage. Regardless of the ultimate validity of morphic resonance, a return to the sense and idea of Nature as alive and animate is absolutely essential to coming into a better relationship with the environment, on which we depend, and therefore is probably essential for our very survival. (Valerian, 1992)

*Negative Intention- is the intention to hold on to the state of negating life and the self, choosing separation. Negative intent will manifest in those choices motivated by pride, self-will and fear which ultimately means the choice to stay separated and alone. (Brennan, 1999-2000 Workbook Junrior, 1996)

*Negative Syndrome-is an aspect of the subjective realm that is defined as a continuum of mental illness and insanity, were the individual is encompassed in fear, hatred and darkness. It is the initiation of the negative evaluation just below the rational line on the affective field, beginning with constructive criticism and continuing through to total apathy. The resulting effect in the life expression of the individual who makes the cause of negative evaluation is the experience of negative self destructive changes within one's mental and physical wellbeing and the generation of low quality problematic inter- personal relationships. (Powers)

*Neurotransmitter-Neurotransmitters are chemicals that allow the movement of information from one neuron across the gap between it and the adjacent neuron. The release of neurotransmitters from one area of a neuron and the recognition of the chemicals by a receptor site on the adjacent neuron causes an electrical reaction that facilitates the release of the neurotransmitter and its movement across the gap.

*Newtonian Physics- presents the view that the world is made of tiny solid building blocks.

*Nichiren Daishonin-(1222-1282) The founder of the Buddhist tradition, that is based on the Lotus Sutra and urges chanting the phrase Nam-myoho-renge-kyo as a daily practice. Nichiren revealed that Nam-myoho-renge-kyo (Myoho-renge-kyo being the title of the Lotus Sutra) represents the essence of the Lotus's teaching. He embodied it in a mandala called the Gohonzon and taught that chanting that phrase with faith in the Gohonzon is the practice that enables people in the present age, the Latter Day of the Law, to attain Buddhahood.

Nichiren was born on the sixteenth day of the second month, 1222, in Tojo Village of Awa Province, Japan. His father was Mikuni no Taifu, and his mother, Umegiku-nyo. His childhood name was Zennichi-maro (also called Zennichi-maru). In 1233 he entered a nearby temple of the Tendai school called Seicho-ji, where he studied both Buddhist and secular teachings under the senior priest Dozen-bo. According to Nichiren's Letter to the Priests of Seicho-ji, written in 1276, Zennichi-maro prayed before a statue of Bodhisattva Space Treasury at Seicho-ji to become the wisest person in Japan. As a result, the letter says, he obtained "a great jewel," or a jewel of wisdom that later enabled him to grasp the essence of all the sutras.

In 1237 he was formally ordained and took the name Zesho-bo Rencho. Soon after, he left for Kamakura, the seat of the shogunate, to further his studies. Thereafter he returned briefly to Seicho-ji and then set out again for such major centers of Buddhist learning as Mount Hiei, Mount Koya, Onjo-ji temple, and other temples in the Kyoto and Nara areas. During these years he studied all of the available sutras and commentaries, as well as the teachings of the different Buddhist schools. He became firmly convinced that the highest of Shakyamuni's teachings is the Lotus Sutra, and that the great pure Law that leads directly to enlightenment in the Latter Day of the Law is implicit in that sutra. He was also convinced that his was the mission of Bodhisattva Superior Practices, who, according to the Lotus Sutra, was entrusted with the task of propagating that Law in the Latter Day. He resolved to declare the sutra's supremacy and point out the misconceptions of the prevailing Buddhist schools, though he knew that the Lotus Sutra predicts its votary will experience severe persecutions.

In 1253 he returned to Seicho-ji. There at noon on the twenty-eighth day of the fourth month, he preached to an assembly of priests and villagers who had gathered to hear the results of his studies. In that first sermon, he declared that the Lotus Sutra is the true teaching of Shakyamuni Buddha, and that its essence, Nam-myoho-renge-kyo, is the very teaching in the Latter Day of the Law that enables all people to attain Buddhahood in this lifetime. On this occasion he renamed himself Nichiren (Sun Lotus). He also severely criticized the widespread Nembutsu (or Pure Land) doctrine as one that drives people into the hell of incessant suffering. TojoKagenobu, the steward of the area and an ardent Nembutsu believer, became furious on hearing this. He ordered his warriors to seize Nichiren, who narrowly managed to escape with the help of the priests, Joken-bo and Gijo-bo, who were his seniors when they were desciples together at Seicho-ji. After converting his parents and giving the Buddhist name Myonichi (Wonderful Sun) to his father and Myoren (Wonderful Lotus) to his mother, he headed for Kamakura to launch his efforts to spread his teaching. In Kamakura he lived in a dwelling at a place called Matsubagayatsu in Nagoe. He devoted the next several years primarily to converting individuals, eventually gaining a number of followers. Among the first priests to become his disciples were Nissho and Nichiro. Laypersons who converted were mostly samurai, including Toki Jonin, Shijo Kingo, Kudo Yoshitaka, and the Ikegami brothers.

Japan at that time was experiencing a succession of unusually severe storms, earthquakes, drought, famine, epidemics, and other disasters. Corpses littered the streets. Government relief measures and the prayers offered by shrines and temples were no help. An earthquake that struck Kamakura in the eighth month of 1257 destroyed the greater part of the city. Nichiren, determined to clarify a solution to these calamities based on Buddhist principles, went to Jisso-ji temple in Suruga Province to do research in its sutra library. During his stay there, Nikko, then a boy of thirteen studying at the nearby Shijuku-in temple, became Nichiren's disciple. He would later become his successor. On the sixteenth day of the seventh month, 1260, Nichiren submitted a treatise titled On Establishing the Correct Teaching for the Peace of the Land to Hojo Tokiyori, the retired regent who was nevertheless the most influential man in the Kamakura shogunate. In that work, he attributed the disasters ravaging the country to slander of the correct teaching and belief in false teachings. In particular, he criticized the dominant Nembutsu school. Of the three calamities and seven disasters described in the sutras, he predicted that the two disasters that had yet to occur-internal strife and foreign invasion-would befall the nation without fail if it persisted in supporting misleading schools. He urged that the one vehicle teaching of the Lotus Sutra be embraced immediately. The submission of On Establishing the Correct Teaching is regarded as the first of his several remonstrations with Japan's rulers.

There was no official response to this document, but a crowd of Nembutsu believers, incited by priests and high government officials, attacked Nichiren's dwelling on the night of the twenty-seventh day of the eighth month. He narrowly escaped with a few disciples and stayed briefly with Toki Jonin in Shimosa Province. His sense of mission, however, would not allow him to remain there long. The next spring Nichiren returned to Kamakura. This time leaders of the Nembutsu priests accused him of defamation, and the shogunate, without trial or further investigation, sentenced him to exile in Ito on the Izu Peninsula.

The boatmen charged with his transport did not take him to Ito, but abandoned him on a beach called Kawana to the mercy of the local inhabitants, many of whom were Nembutsu believers and were in any case hostile to exiles. Nichiren was sheltered for a time by a fisherman named Funamori Yasaburo and his wife. Later Nichiren won the favor of the steward of Ito when he successfully prayed for the steward's recovery from a serious illness. Nichiren was pardoned and returned to Kamakura in the second month of 1263. Concerned about his aged mother (his father had died in 1258), Nichiren returned to his native Awa in the autumn of 1264. He found his mother critically ill. He prayed for her, and she recovered and lived four more years. He stayed in Awa for awhile to conduct propagation activities.

On the eleventh day of the eleventh month, while still in Awa, he set out with a group of followers to visit Kudo Yoshitaka, one of his samurai believers, at Yoshitaka's invitation. En route, Nichiren and his party were ambushed by TojoKagenobu and his men at a place called Komatsubara. Nichiren's disciple Kyonin-bo was killed, and Kudo Yoshitaka, who came rushing to the scene, died of wounds he suffered in the fight. Nichiren sustained a sword cut on his forehead and a broken hand. This incident is called the Komatsubara Persecution.

During the next three years or so, Nichiren devoted himself to propagation in Awa, Kazusa, Shimosa, and Hitachi provinces, and then returned to Kamakura. Early in 1268, an official letter from the Mongol Empire arrived in Japan with a demand that Japan acknowledge fealty to it or prepare to be invaded. The arrival of the letter from the Mongols substantiated Nichiren's earlier prophecy of foreign invasion.

In the fourth month Nichiren sent his newly written rationale for having completed the treatise On Establishing the Correct Teaching to a government official named Hogan, pointing out that the prediction made in the treatise was beginning to come true and urging the shogunate to heed his admonitions. On the eleventh day of the tenth month, he sent eleven letters to influential political and religious leaders, including the regent Hojo Tokimune, urging them to abandon their faith in erroneous teachings and demanding the opportunity for a public religious debate. There was no response.

In 1271 the country was troubled by persistent drought, and the shogunate ordered Ryokan of Gokuraku-ji temple to pray for rain. Hearing of this, Nichiren sent Ryokan a written challenge, offering to become his disciple if Ryokan succeeded; on the other hand, if Ryokan failed, he should become Nichiren's disciple. Ryokan readily agreed, but despite his prayers and those of hundreds of attendant priests, no rain fell. Far from keeping his promise, he vindictively began to spread false rumors about Nichiren, using his influence among the wives and widows of shogunate officials. On the tenth day of the ninth month, Nichiren was summoned to court and interrogated by Hei no Saemon, the deputy chief of the Office of Military and Police Affairs (the chief being the regent himself). He reemphasized the errors of the True Word (Shingon), Zen, and Nembutsu schools and repeated his prediction that the country would face ruin if it continued to reject the correct teaching.

On the evening of the twelfth day of the ninth month, Hei no Saemon, with a large group of his soldiers, attacked and arrested Nichiren. As he later wrote, Nichiren said to Hei no Saemon at the time: "Nichiren is the pillar and beam of Japan. Doing away with me is toppling the pillar of Japan!". Hei no Saemon then maneuvered to have Nichiren beheaded and had him taken late that night to the execution grounds at Tatsunokuchi. Just as the executioner had raised his sword to strike, a brilliant object shot across the sky, illuminating everyone like bright moonlight. Nichiren wrote later: "The executioner fell on his face, his eyes blinded. The soldiers were filled with panic". In the end, they abandoned the execution. Nichiren wrote about this incident, called the Tatsunokuchi Persecution, in The Opening of the Eyes: "On the twelfth day of the ninth month of last year [1271], between the hours of the rat and the ox [11:00 P.M. to 3:00 A.M.], this person named Nichiren was beheaded. It is his soul that has come to this island of Sado and, in the second month of the following year, snowbound, is writing this to send to his close disciples". Nichikan (1665-1726), the twenty-sixth chief priest of Taiseki-ji temple, interpreted this passage to mean that the ordinary person Nichiren died at Tatsunokuchi, but the Buddha of the Latter Day of the Law Nichiren survived. This is called "casting off the transient [status] and revealing the true [identity] (Jpn hosshaku-kem-pon)." After this, Nichiren began to inscribe the object of devotion known as the Gohonzon.

On the tenth day of the tenth month, after an almost one-month stay in Echi in Sagami Province, Nichiren left under escort for Sado Island, his designated place of exile, and arrived at Tsukahara on Sado on the first day of the eleventh month. There he was assigned as his dwelling a dilapidated hut in a graveyard, exposed to the wind and snow. On the sixteenth day of the first month in the following year, several hundred priests from Sado and the mainland came to confront him in religious debate. In what is known as the Tsukahara Debate, Nichiren refuted those priests and won converts. In the second month of that year, Nichiren's prediction of internal strife came true when Hojo Tokisuke, an elder half brother of Regent Hojo Tokimune, made an abortive attempt to seize power. In the fourth month Nichiren was transferred from Tsukahara to the more comfortable residence of the lay priest Ichinosawa. While on Sado he wrote many of his most important works, including The Opening of the Eyes, The Object of Devotion for Observing the Mind, The Heritage of the Ultimate Law of Life, The True Aspect of All Phenomena, The Entity of the Mystic Law, On the Buddha's Prophecy, and On Practicing the Buddha's Teachings.

In the second month of 1274, the shogunate issued a pardon for Nichiren, and he returned to Kamakura the next month. On the eighth day of the fourth month, Hei no Saemon summoned Nichiren and, in a deferential manner, asked his opinion regarding the impending Mongol invasion. Nichiren said that it would occur within the year and reiterated that this calamity was the result of slandering the correct teaching. On this occasion the shogunate offered to build him a large temple and establish him on an equal footing with all the other Buddhist schools, but Nichiren refused. He instead again refuted the errors of the shogunate.

The shogunate continued its support of the True Word and other schools. Convinced that he had done all he could to warn the nation's leaders of their religious errors and of what would ensue as a result, Nichiren now turned his efforts to ensuring the correct transmission of his teachings to posterity. In keeping with an old maxim that a worthy man who warns his sovereign three times and still is not heeded should withdraw to a mountain forest, he left Kamakura on the twelfth day of the fifth month, and went to take up residence at the foot of Mount Minobu in Kai Province. There he gave lectures on the Lotus Sutra and devoted himself to training his disciples. He also continued to write, producing such important documents as One Taking the Essence of the Lotus Sutra, The Selection of the Time, and On Repaying Debts of Gratitude.

In the tenth month of 1274, the Mongols launched a massive attack against the southern Japanese islands of Iki and Tsushima and advanced to Kyushu. Japanese losses were staggering, but one night when the Mongol forces returned to their battleships, an unexpected storm arose and heavily damaged the Mongol fleet, which then withdrew. In the fourth month of the next year, however, the Mongols sent an envoy relaying a threat of another invasion if the Japanese government did not acknowledge fealty to their empire. During this period, Nichiren was busy at Minobu writing letters, training his disciples, and lecturing on the Lotus Sutra. Nikko assumed active leadership in disseminating Nichiren's teachings, concentrating his efforts in Kai, Izu, and Suruga provinces. These activities led to an increase in converts among both the priesthood and laity, and eventually to more oppression. In Atsuhara Village of the Fuji area, in particular, believers were repeatedly threatened and harassed, and some were finally executed. In what later became known as the Atsuhara Persecution, twenty believers, all farmers, were arrested on false charges on the twenty-first day of the ninth month, 1279. Though tortured to force them to recant their beliefs, not one of the twenty farmers yielded. Three of them were beheaded on the fifteenth day of the tenth month (another account, the eighth day of the fourth month, 1280). Nichiren, seeing that his followers now had the strength to uphold their faith even at the cost of their lives, determined that the time had come to fulfill the ultimate purpose of his life. On the twelfth day of the tenth month, 1279, he inscribed the object of devotion (known as the Dai-Gohonzon) and dedicated it for the attainment of Buddhahood by all humanity.

Subsequently, his health began to fail. Sensing that death was near, Nichiren designated Nikko as his successor in a transfer document dated the ninth month of 1282. On the eighth day of the ninth month, he left Minobu at the urging of his followers to visit a hot spring in Hitachi. When he reached the residence of Ikegami Munenaka at Ikegami in Musashi Province, he realized that his death was imminent. There he lectured for his followers on On Establishing the Correct Teaching. On the eighth day of the tenth month, he named six senior priests and entrusted them with the responsibility for propagation after his death. Early on the morning of the thirteenth day of the tenth month, he appointed Nikko as the chief priest of Kuon-ji temple in Minobu, directing all believers to follow him. He died that morning, in the company of his disciples, both priests and laity. (Nichiren Shoshu Internation Center, 1983)

*Nine consciousnesses- Nine kinds of discernment. "Consciousness" is the translation of the Sanskrit vijnana, which means discernment. The nine consciousnesses are (1) sight-conscious-ness (Skt chakshur-vijnana), (2) hearing-consciousness (shrota-vijnana), (3) smell-consciousness (ghrana-vijnana), (4) taste-consciousness (jihvavijnana), (5) touch-consciousness (kaya-vijnana), (6) mind-consciousness (mano-vijnana), (7) mano-consciousness (mano-vijnana), (8) alaya-con-sciousness (alaya-vijnana), and (9) amala-consciousness (amala-vijnana). (The Sanskrit is the same for both the sixth and seventh consciousnesses.)

The first five consciousnesses correspond to the five senses of sight, hearing, smell, taste, and touch. The sixth consciousness integrates the perceptions of the five senses into coherent images and makes judgments about the external world. In contrast with the first six consciousnesses, which deal with the external world, the seventh, or mano-consciousness, corresponds to the inner spiritual world. Awareness of and attachment to the self are said to originate from the mano-consciousness, as does the ability to distinguish between good and evil. The eighth, or alaya consciousness, exists in what modern psychology calls the unconscious; all experiences of present and previous lifetimes-collectively called karma-are stored there. The alaya-consciousness receives the results of one's good and evil deeds and stores them as karmic potentials or "seeds," which then produce the rewards of either happiness or suffering accordingly. Hence it was rendered as "storehouse consciousness" in Chinese. The alaya-consciousness thus forms the framework of individual existence. The Dharma Characteristics (Chin Fa-hsiang; Jpn Hosso) school regards the eighth consciousness as the source of all spiritual and physical phenomena. The Summary of the Mahayana (She-lun; Shoron) school, the T'ien-t'ai school, and the Flower Garland (Hua-yen; Kegon) school postulate a ninth consciousness, called amala-consciousness, which lies below the alaya-consciousness and remains free from all karmic impurity. This ninth consciousness is defined as the basis of all life's functions. Hence it was rendered as "fundamental pure consciousness" in Chinese.

*Nichiren Shoshu- is the 750 year old orthodox Buddhist denomination centered at Head Temple, Taisekiji, at the foot of Mt. Fuji in Japan. Nichiren Shoshu has temples and centers worldwide and actively propagates the teachings of the True Buddha, Nichiren Daishonin, who made His advent in Japan in 1222. The practice of Nichiren Shoshu brings powerful benefits and positive changes to the lives of those who practice it. The ultimate goals are the attainment of enlightenment by the individual and, through widely spreading True Buddhism, the establishment of a purified world where all people can enjoy happy lives together.

The daily practice consists of chanting Nam-Myoho-Renge-Kyo and reciting portions of the Lotus Sutra to the fundamental Object of Worship called the Gohonzon.

*Nin Honzon- the object of worship as the person. Nichiren Daishonin.

*Ninpo Ikka- the entity of the fusion of the person (Buddha) and the Law of Nam myoho renge kyo; the Gohonzon.

*Ongi Kuden- Nichiren's oral teachings on the Lotus Sutra, recorded and compiled by his disciple and successor Nikko. At Minobu in Kai Province, Japan, Nichiren gave a series of lectures for his disciples on important sentences and phrases from the Lotus Sutra. This work, dated the first month of 1278, consists of two parts and reveals the essential principles of Nichiren's teachings. When explaining the meaning of a passage of the sutra, he cited as references the major works of T'ien-t'ai and Miao-lo; he then interpreted the passage to clarify essential tenets of his teaching. The Record of the Orally Transmitted Teachings begins with a lecture on the meaning of Nam-myoho-renge-kyo and then proceeds through each of the twenty-eight chapters of the Lotus Sutra as well as the Immeasurable Meanings Sutra and the Universal Worthy Sutra. It concludes with two separate lectures: "The Essential Passage in Each of the Twenty-eight Chapters of the Lotus Sutra" and "All the Twenty-eight Chapters of the Lotus Sutra Are Nam-myoho-renge-kyo." (Nichiren Shoshu Internation Center, 1983)

*Pookrum, Jewel M.D.- Founder & Director of the 'Civilized Medicine Institute' where clinical medicine and Holistic practice combine. Trained as a Surgeon, Gynecologist and Holistic/ General Practitioner she is also a lecturer and author of 'Vitamins and Minerals from A to Z.' Her specialty is Intrinsic Stem Cell Activation, Intrinsic Tissue Regeneration, Integrative Medicine, Human Ecology Medicine, Integrative Gynecology and Integrative Oncology.

*Positive Aura- a continuum of mental health and well being, beginning with a positive evaluation, acknowledgment through infinite affection. Defined as a continuum of love, faith and light, the anti-thesis of the negative syndrome, living in this state is very difficult by nature requiring effort in a direction which defies the logic of our very basic nature. However, living in the positive aura generates an environment of positive body chemistry (alkaline pH) and exerts a positive atmosphere (energy field) positively affective those around you. (Powers)

*Positive intention- is the characteristic to choose the unitive state even if there is a strong impulse to do otherwise. It manifest in decisions that are motivated by love, truth, integrity, courage, harmony and joy. It requires the individual to remain unified within one's being and hold that unified consciousness within the interactions with others, the intent for the flow of the life force to occur from essence. (Brennan, 1999-2000 Workbook Junior, 1996)

*Prayer- in Buddhism it means to make promise or pledge, not a request to be given something. You become a person who can handle all of their problems. As a result of chanting Daimoku, you understand what you must do and never lose ones' conviction in any type of situation.

*Sango funi- Also, three types of action. Activities carried out with one's body, mouth, and mind, i.e., deeds, words, and thoughts. Buddhism holds that karma, good or evil, is created by these three types of action-mental, verbal, and physical. Here "action" is the translation of the Sanskrit karman.

*Seven Kinds of gems- Also, seven treasures or seven kinds of gems. Precious substances mentioned in the sutras. The list differs among the Buddhist scriptures. According to the Lotus Sutra, the seven are gold, silver, lapis lazuli, seashell, agate, pearl, and carnelian. In the "Treasure Tower" (eleventh) chapter of the sutra, the treasure tower adorned with these seven kinds of treasures appears from beneath the earth. In a letter known as On the Treasure Tower, Nichiren associates the seven kinds of treasures that adorn the treasure tower with the seven elements of practice, writing: "It is the treasure tower adorned with the seven kinds of treasures-hearing the correct teaching, believing it, keeping the precepts, engaging in meditation, practicing assiduously, renouncing one's attachments, and reflecting on oneself ." Seven indispensable elements of Buddhist practice, which are compared to treasures. They are hearing the correct teaching, believing it, keeping the precepts, engaging in meditation, practicing assiduously, renouncing one's attachments, and reflecting on oneself. (Nichiren Shoshu Internation Center, 1983)

*Shakyamuni- Also known as Gautama Buddha, the founder of Buddhism. "Shakyamuni" means "sage of the Shakyas," Shakya being the name of the tribe or clan to which his family belonged. Opinions differ concerning the dates of his birth and death. According to Buddhist tradition in China and Japan, he was born on the eighth day of the fourth month of 1029 B.C.E. and died on the fifteenth day of the second month of 949 B.C.E., but recent studies have him living nearly five hundred years later. The view prevalent among scholars is that Shakyamuni lived from about 560 to about 480 B.C.E., though some scholars hold that he lived from about 460 to about 380 B.C.E. He was the son of Shuddhodana, the king of the Shakyas, a small tribe whose kingdom was located in the foothills of the Himalayas south of what is now central Nepal. Shakyamuni's family name was Gautama (Best Cow), and his childhood or given name was Siddhartha (Goal Achieved), though some scholars say the latter is a title bestowed on him by later Buddhists in honor of the enlightenment he attained.

According to the Buddhist scriptures, Shakyamuni was born in Lumbini Gardens, in what is now Rummindei in southern Nepal. His mother, Maya, died on the seventh day after his birth, and he was raised thereafter by her younger sister Mahaprajapati. In his boyhood and adolescence, he is said to have excelled in both learning and the martial arts. Though raised amid the luxuries of the royal palace, he seems to have very soon become aware of and been profoundly troubled by the problem of human suffering. As a young man, he married the beautiful Yashodhara, who bore him a son, Rahula. He became increasingly possessed, however, by a longing to abandon the secular world and go out in search of a solution to the inherent sufferings of life. Buddhist scriptures describe four encounters, which served to awaken in him an awareness of these four sufferings common to all people-birth, aging, sickness, and death-and a desire to seek their solution. Eventually he renounced his princely status and embarked on the life of a religious mendicant.

Having left the palace of the Shakyas at Kapilavastu, Shakyamuni traveled south to Rajagriha, the capital of the kingdom of Magadha, where he studied first with Alara Kalama and then with Uddaka Ramaputta, both teachers of yogic meditation. Though he quickly mastered their respective forms of meditation, he did not find the answers to his questions in these disciplines. Leaving Rajagriha, he proceeded to the bank of the Nairanjana River near the village of Uruvilva, where he began to engage in ascetic practices in the company of other ascetics. For six years, he subjected himself to disciplines of appalling severity, far surpassing those of his companions, but he found it entirely impossible to reach emancipation through such self-mortification and eventually rejected these practices as well. To restore his body, which had been weakened by long fasting, he accepted milk curds offered him by a girl named Sujata. Then, near the city of Gaya, he seated himself under a pipal tree and entered meditation. There he attained an awakening, or enlightenment, to the true nature of life and all things. It was because of this enlightenment that he came to be called Buddha, or "Awakened One." According to Buddhist tradition in China and Japan, Siddhartha renounced secular life at age nineteen and attained enlightenment at thirty. (Modern scholars generally place these ages at twenty-nine and thirty-five, respectively.) The pipal tree was later called the bodhi tree, bodhi meaning enlightenment, and the site itself came to be called Buddhagaya.

After his awakening, Shakyamuni is said to have remained for a while beneath the tree, rejoicing in his emancipation yet troubled by the knowledge of how difficult it would be to communicate what he had realized to others. For a while, he vacillated as to whether he should attempt to teach others what he had achieved. At length, however, he resolved that he would strive to do so, so that the way to liberation from the sufferings of birth and death would be open to all people. First he made his way to Deer Park in Varanasi, where he preached and converted five ascetics who had formerly been his companions.

After that, Shakyamuni's efforts to propagate his teaching advanced rapidly. In Varanasi he converted Yashas, the son of a rich man, and about sixty others. Then he headed back toward the site of his enlightenment, the village of Uruvilvanear Gaya. There he converted three brothers- Uruvilva Kashyapa, Nadi Kashyapa, and Gaya

Kashyapa-who were leaders among Brahman ascetics, along with their one thousand followers. The Buddha then set out for Rajagriha in Magadha, where he converted its king, Bimbisara, as well as Shariputra and Maudgalyayana, who would become two of the Buddha's leading disciples. The latter two were at that time followers of Sanjaya, one of the six non-Buddhist teachers. Together with Shariputra and Maudgalyayana, all of Sanjaya's followers-said to number 250-forsook him and entered the Buddhist Order. Mahakashyapa also became another of the Buddha's disciples in Rajagriha shortly thereafter.

The Buddha made several trips to his childhood home, Kapilavastu, resulting in the conversion of many people, including his younger half brother Nanda, his son Rahula, his cousins Ananda, Aniruddha, and Devadatta, and a barber named Upali. Shakyamuni's father, Shuddhodana, and his former wife, Yashodhara, are also said to have embraced the Buddhist teachings. The Buddha permitted his foster mother, Mahaprajapati, to enter the Buddhist Order, and thus the order of Buddhist nuns was established. At that time there was a powerful kingdom called Kosala that rivaled Magadha. In Shravasti, the capital of Kosala, a wealthy and influential merchant named Sudatta became the Buddha's lay follower and patron. He had met Shakyamuni while on business in Rajagriha and converted. Sudatta built Jetavana Monastery in Shravasti as an offering to the Buddha, and Shakyamuni is said to have spent twenty-five rainy seasons at this monastery with his disciples. Prasenajit, the king of Kosala, also became a Buddhist.

In the fifty years (forty-five according to modern scholars) from the time of his awakening until he died, Shakyamuni continued to travel through much of India to disseminate his teachings. Among the places where he concentrated his efforts were the cities of Rajagriha in Magadha; Shravasti in Kosala; Vaishali, capital of the Vriji confederacy; and Kaushambi, the capital of Vatsa. The Buddha's disciples in the monastic order were also active in spreading his teachings. Mahakatyayana was a native of the kingdom of Avanti in the western part of central India and made several converts there, including the king. Purna propagated Shakyamuni's teachings in Sunaparanta in western India north of present-day Bombay.

Thus even during Shakyamuni's lifetime, his teachings spread not only in central India but also to more remote areas, and people of all classes converted to Buddhism. The new religious movement, however, was perceived by many as a threat to the old Brahmanic order, and in the course of his efforts Shakyamuni personally underwent numerous hardships, representative of which are the so-called nine great ordeals. Persevering in the face of adversity, he continued to preach his message of emancipation, expounding the teachings in various ways according to the circumstances and capacity of his listeners. The teachings he left are so numerous that they later came to be called the eighty thousand teachings.

Shakyamuni died at age eighty. The year before his death, he stayed at Gridhrakuta (Eagle Peak) near Rajagriha. Then he set out on his last journey, proceeding northward across the Ganges River to Vaishali. He spent the rainy season in Beluva, a village near Vaishali. During this retreat he became seriously ill, but recovered and continued to preach in many villages. Eventually he came to a place called Pavain Malla. There he again became ill after eating a meal prepared as an offering by the village blacksmith, Chunda. Despite his pain, he continued his journey until he reached Kushinagara, where in a grove of sal trees he calmly lay down and spoke his last words. He admonished his disciples, saying: "You must not think that your teacher's words are no more, or that you are left without a teacher. The teachings and precepts I have expounded to you shall be your teacher." His final words are said to have been, "Decay is inherent in all composite things. Work out your salvation with diligence." His body was received by the Mallas of Kushinagara and cremated seven days later. The ashes were divided into eight parts, and eight stupas were erected to enshrine them. Two more stupas were built to house the vessel used in the cremation and the ashes of the fire. In the same year, the First Buddhist Council was held in the Cave of the Seven Leaves near Rajagriha to compile Shakyamuni's teachings. (Nichiren Shoshu International Center, 1983)

*Shoho- the living self or subjective world the two are inseparable phases of the same entity of life.

*Six transcendental powers-Also, six supernatural powers. Powers that Buddhas, bodhisattvas, and arhats are said to possess. They are (1) the power to be anywhere at will, (2) the power to see anything anywhere, (3) the power to hear any sound anywhere, (4) the power to know the thoughts of all other minds, (5) the power to know past lives, and (6) the power to eradicate illusions and earthly desires. (Nichiren Shoshu International Center, 1983)

*Soul Seat- corresponds to our emotions and spiritual longing that leads us throughout our life. This point along the hara line brings the passion we have to accomplish great things and is specific to our life task. (Brennan, Light Emerging, 1993)

*Surrender- is to deliver up or give over to a higher imperative, (as a spiritual process) requires that an individual surrenders to the divine essence that we are, all that there is and we are moment to moment. The proper function of the ego is to negotiate the delicate balance between the inner and outer worlds. The personality develops around this interface, yet as we develop spiritually this becomes our biggest hindrance and obstacle. This is because as the force of our core essence evolves the greater the resistance the ego/personality holds onto its limited view of reality and itself, making surrender an essential aspect of spiritual development. (Brennan, 1999-2000 Workbook Junior, 1996)

*Tan Tien- this is the point of our will to live in the physical body located approximately 2 1/2 inches below the navel in the hara dimension. It is from this point that the individual draws up the physical body from the body of mother earth. The healer uses this point to connect to a great deal of power to regenerate from the molten core by extending the hara line down into the earth. (Brennan, 1999-2000 Workbook Junior, 1996)

*Ten Evil acts- Evils enumerated in the Buddhist scriptures. They are the three physical evils of killing, stealing, and sexual misconduct; the four verbal evils of lying, flattery or indiscriminate and irresponsible speech, defamation, and duplicity; and the three mental evils of greed, anger, and foolishness or the holding of mistaken views. From the viewpoint of the precepts, the ten evil acts constitute violations of the ten good precepts, which proscribe those acts; they are the opposite of the ten good acts, which are to refrain from the ten evil acts. (Nichiren Shoshu Internation Center, 1983)

* The lower six worlds- are controlled by earthly desires and are governed by an ever changing environment.

*Three obstacles and four Devils- Various obstacles and hindrances to the practice of Buddhism. They are listed in the Nirvana Sutra and The Treatise on the Great Perfection of Wisdom. The three obstacles are (1) the obstacle of earthly desires, or obstacles arising from the three poisons of greed, anger, and foolishness; (2) the obstacle of karma, obstacles due to bad karma created by committing any of the five cardinal sins or ten evil acts; and (3) the obstacle of retribution, obstacles caused by the negative karmic effects of actions in the three evil paths. In a letter he addressed to the Ikegami brothers in 1275, Nichiren states, "The obstacle of earthly desires is the impediments to one's practice that arise from greed, anger, foolishness, and the like; the obstacle of karma is the hindrances presented by one's wife or children; and the obstacle of retribution is the hindrances caused by one's sovereign or parents."

The four devils are (1) the hindrance of the five components, obstructions caused by one's physical and mental functions; (2) the hindrance of earthly desires, obstructions arising from the three poisons; (3) the hindrance of death, meaning one's own untimely death obstructing one's practice of Buddhism, or the premature death of another practitioner causing one to doubt; and (4) the hindrance of the devil king, who is said to assume various forms or take possession of others in order to cause one to discard one's Buddhist practice. This hindrance is regarded as the most difficult to overcome. T'ien-t'ai (538-597) states in Great Concentration and Insight: "As practice progresses and understanding grows, the three obstacles and four devils emerge in confusing form, vying with one another to interfere.... . One should be neither influenced nor fright-ened by them. If one falls under their influence, one will be led into the paths of evil. If one is frightened by them, one will be prevented from practicing the correct teaching." (Nichiren Shoshu International Center, 1983)

*Three poisons- Greed, anger, and foolishness. The fundamental evils inherent in life, that gives rise to human suffering. In The Treatise on the Great Perfection of Wisdom, the three poisons are regarded as the source of all illusions and earthly desires. The three poisons are so called because they pollute people's lives and work to prevent them from turning their hearts and minds to goodness. The Words and

Phrases of the Lotus Sutra by T'ien-t'ai speaks of the three poisons as the underlying cause of the three calamities of famine, war, and pestilence, stating: "Because anger increases in intensity, armed strife occurs. Because greed increases in intensity, famine arises. Because foolishness increases in intensity, pestilence breaks out. And because these three calamities occur, earthly desires grow more numerous and powerful than ever, and false views increasingly flourish." In the "Simile and Parable" (third) chapter of the Lotus Sutra, Shakyamuni says to Shariputra, "He [the Thus Come One] is born into the threefold world, a burning house, rotten and old, in order to save living beings from the fires of birth, aging, sickness, and death, care, suffering, stupidity, misunderstanding, and the three poisons; to teach and convert them and enable them to attain supreme perfect enlightenment." (Nichiren Shoshu Internation Center, 1983)

*Three types of auric field interaction-

    1. Bioplasmic streamers

    2. Harmonic induction

    3. Cords

*Transcendence- is the expansion of awareness and self-identity to higher levels of our being; inner duality subsides, the mind becomes clearer, more creative process is released within us. Our increased energy automatically brings us into direct experience of our higher being. (Brennan, 1999-2000 Workbook Junior, 1996)

*Transference- the process when attention is focused on the experienced events and then the experience is retained as a habitual form of memory aligned in a stimulus-response fashion, where emotions are an enhancer of the storage process for responses and the individual cannot experience the event in current time for itself. They get caught up in the event and react according to habitual response patterns, which must be unlearned if they wish to develop non-dual conscious perception of events as they really exist. All events are in fact neutral in content and meaning, yet the individual gives an event meaning and projects that meaning on the event. (Valerian, 1992)

*Transfiguration- is the process of entering into at-one-ment with divine essence. Holding clear intentionality aligned with divinity brings us to greater experience of our Inner Divine Essence, and we begin to enter a profound awareness of the true nature of what was perceived as boundary. (Brennan, 1999-2000 Workbook Junior, 1996)

*Transformation- is the process of exploring our inner landscape, our past and its effect on our functioning right now. Our past includes childhood, inter-utero experiences, between life experiences, and past life experiences. (Brennan, 1999-2000 Workbook Junior, 1996)

*Twelve link chain of cause and effect-Also, twelve nidanas or twelve-linked chain of dependent origination. An early doctrine of Buddhism showing the causal relationship between ignorance and suffering. The Sanskrit word nidana means cause or cause of existence. Shakyamuni is said to have taught the twelve-linked chain of causation in answer to the question of why people have to experience the sufferings of aging and death. Each link in the chain is a cause that leads to the next. The first link in the chain is ignorance (Skt avidya), which gives rise to (2) action (samskara) (also, volition or karmic action); (3) action causes consciousness (vijnana), or the function to discern; (4) consciousness causes name and form (nama-rupa), or spiritual and material objects of discernment; (5) name and form cause the six sense organs (shad-ayatana); (6) the six sense organs cause contact (sparsha); (7) contact causes sensation (vedana); (8) sensation causes desire (trishna); (9) desire causes attachment (upadana); (10) attachment causes existence (bhava); (11) existence causes birth (jati); and (12) birth causes aging and death (jara-marana).

The twelve-linked chain of causation is seen in two ways: the way of transmigration and the way of emancipation. From the viewpoint of the way of transmigration, ignorance gives rise to action, action causes consciousness, etc.; finally, birth causes aging and death as explained above. Thus one is caught in the cycle of delusion and suffering. On the other hand, from the viewpoint of the way of emancipation, if ignorance is wiped out, so is action; if action is wiped out, so is consciousness, etc.; finally, if birth is wiped out, so are aging and suffering. In short, if one eliminates ignorance, which is the source of suffering, one becomes free from the cycle of delusion and suffering, or attains nirvana.

The Great Commentary on the Abhidharma, a text of the Sarvastivada school, views the twelve-linked chain of causation as operating over the three existences of life, meaning one's past, present, and future existences. (1) Ignorance and (2) action are together interpreted as the causes created in a past life; (3) consciousness through (7) sensation, as the effects manifest in the present life; (8) desire through (10) existence, as the causes created in the present life; and (11) birth and (12) aging and death, as the effects manifest in the next life. Aging and death in this life are thus the results of causes formed in a previous life. (Nichiren Shoshu Internation Center, 1983)

*Yujitsu chapter (15th) –the bodhisattvas of the earth appeared in this chapter of the Lotus sutra.

*Zuitai- the Buddha's teachings in accordance with the minds of others.

*Zuiji- The Buddha's direct preaching of his enlightenment, irrespective of the capacity of his listeners. It contrasts with "preaching in accordance with the minds of others," or preaching that accords with the capacities of the listeners. These two concepts come from the Mahaparinirvana Sutra. In Great Concentration and Insight and The Profound Meaning of the Lotus Sutra, T'ien-t'ai (538-597) categorizes the Lotus Sutra as a teaching that accords with the Buddha's own mind and the other sutras as teachings that accord with the minds of others. He defines the Lotus Sutra as a teaching that directly reveals the Buddha's enlightenment regardless of the people's varying capacities to understand it, and the other sutras as expedient means, taught in accordance with the capacity of the people.

In The Outstanding Principles of the Lotus Sutra, Dengyo (767-822), the founder of the Japanese Tendai School, adheres to T'ien-t'ai's interpretation of the Lotus Sutra as a teaching in which the Buddha directly revealed what he had attained. In A Comparison of the Lotus and Other Sutras, Nichiren says: "The teachings expounded in accordance with the people's capacity are the sutras that the Buddha preached in response to the wishes of the people of the nine worlds, just as a wise father instructs an ignorant son in a way suited to the child's understanding. On the other hand, the teaching expounded in accordance with the Buddha's enlightenment is the sutra that the Buddha preached directly from the world of Buddha hood, just as a sage father guides his ignorant son to his own understanding." (Nichiren Shoshu Internation Center, 1983)

Bibliography

Baines, J. (1993). *The Science of Love.* New York: John Baines Institute, Inc.

Brennan, B. (1996). *1999-2000 Workbook Junior.* East Hampton: BBSH.

Brennan, B. (1988). *Hands of Light.* New York: Bantam Books.

Brennan, B. (1993). *Light Emerging.* New York: Bantam Books.

Jewell Pookrum M.D., P. (1999, April). The Seven Ciruits of Brain Function- Lecture. Washington, DC, USA.

Maps of India. (2008). Retrieved April 5, 2008, from maps of india: http://india.mapsofindia.com/the-country/ancient-history/kushan-empire.html

Medicine, U. N. (n.d.). *Handbook.* Retrieved April 5, 2008, from Genetics Home Reference: http://ghr.nlm.nih.gov/handbook/basics/dna

Nichiren Shoshu Internation Center. (1983). *A Dictionary of Buddhist Terms and Concepts.* Tokyo.

Powers, D. M. (n.d.). Creative Selling. Saltlake, Utau, USA.

Sen-shou, L. (2008). *99fall.* Retrieved April 5, 2008, from http://taipei.tzuchi.org.tw/tzquart/99fall/qf99-12.htm

The Gosho Translation Committee. (1992,91,90, 89,88,87,86). *The Major Writings of Nichiren Daishonin.* Tokyo, Japan: Nichiren Shoshu International Center.

Toda, J. (1968). *Lecture on the Sutra.* Tokyo: The Seikyo Press.

Valerian, V. (1992). *The Psychosocial, Chemical, Biological and Electromagnetic Manipulation of Human Consciousness.* Yelm: Leading Edge Research Group.

Wikipedia. (2008). Retrieved April 5, 2008, from Wikipedia: http://en.wikipedia.org

www.ingramcontent.com/pod-product-compliance
Lightning Source LLC
Chambersburg PA
CBHW041532220426
43662CB00002B/39